Praise for
Nourishing a Culture of Leadership

I have been part of a learning journey with Birgitt since 2000. In all our encounters she brings authenticity, shares profound wisdom, and is clear about her position. *The Genuine Contact Way: Nourishing a Culture of Leadership* invites you to step into your power as the leader of your life, including your professional life. This explorative journey will be both challenging and difficult at times, but I highly recommend it. We need you and many others working from your potential to meet the challenges of the world today.

—Thomas Herrmann, Sweden

The Genuine Contact Way provides a window into the thinking, values, and journey with genuine contact both as a personal practice and as a way of supporting organizations and individuals in creating healthy, effective, and life-nourishing ways of being. The beauty of the book is that in telling her story in this highly personal way both the foundations of the Genuine Contact way and how it can be applied in practice are reflected upon. It was a joy to read. Part of the beauty of the book is that, like so many experiences I've had with the Genuine Contact program and its international community of professionals, the book helped me to deepen my understanding of my unique journey with genuine contact and how this journey has enhanced me both as a professional and in my larger life.

—Doris Gottlieb, the Netherlands

I love *The Genuine Contact Way* because it starts at the very beginning: Birgitt displays the foundations of her life and work—her worldview and the key beliefs based upon that worldview. In sharing her story, she is offering many ways to support personal as well as organizational development and growth. One outcome is the Genuine Contact program, with highly effective tools and processes for assisting organizations in being successful. Very inspiring and highly recommended for leaders and consultants who want to really make a difference!

—Monika Himpelmann, Austria

As a person who is deeply involved in the work of helping organizations and organizational leaders move in new directions, I highly endorse *The Genuine Contact Way*. This book helps individuals, leaders, and organizations look beyond the symptoms and problems that slow the forward progress of an organization and its leaders. If offers a way for leaders and organizations to look below the surface and connect to the deepest wisdom of people and institutions; develop practices for individual and organizational health and well-being; and attend to the grief and conflict that is always present in growing and changing organizations. It provides simple frameworks for doing the deep authentic work required for genuine contact and authentic living. I believe *The Genuine Contact Way* will empower people and organizations to discern their divine purpose and develop practices that will support their divine calling.

—Rev. Michael Vinson, USA

After university I took Birgitt's workshops because she is my mother and I wanted to be able to explain what she did for a living. I also had an idea that what she did would help me in my business. As I took the courses I realized that what she taught was applicable to all aspects of life and that she had used many of the principles to raise my siblings and me. These teachings were her way of teaching each of us to find our own leadership.

—David Bolton, Canada

THE GENUINE CONTACT WAY

Nourishing a Culture
of Leadership

Birgitt Williams

Birgitt Williams

Copyright © 2010, 2014 by Dalar International Consultancy

All rights reserved. Except as permitted under the U.S. Copyright Act of 1976, no part of this publication may be reproduced, distributed or transmitted in any form or by any means, or stored in a database or retrieval system, without the prior written permission of the publisher.

(birgitt@dalarinternational.com)

Limits of Liability and Disclaimer of Warranty:

The authors and/or publisher shall not be liable for your misuse of this material. The contents are strictly for informational and educational purposes only.

Warning—Disclaimer:
The purpose of this book is to educate and entertain. The authors and/or publisher do not guarantee that anyone following these techniques, suggestions, tips, ideas, or strategies will become successful. The author and/or publisher shall have neither liability nor responsibility to anyone with respect to any loss or damage caused, or alleged to be caused, directly or indirectly by the information contained in this book. Further, readers should be aware that Internet websites listed in this work may have changed or disappeared between when this work was written and when it is read.

Printed and bound in the United States of America

Published by DALAR
PO Box 19373, Raleigh, NC, 27619
www.genuinecontactway.com

First edition 2010
Second edition July 2014
Library of Congress Control Number: 2014913709
ISBN: 978-1-926934-31-0

Dedication

This book is dedicated, with heartfelt gratitude, to the team that has surrounded me with their love, encouragement, wisdom, and numerous contributions through the development of the Genuine Contact Way project and in life. I am grateful to you from my heart overflowing with love.

Ward Williams, Rachel Amanda, Laura Bolton, David Bolton, Aaron Bolton

I give special thanks to the international community of Genuine Contact professionals, dear friends of my heart, who have shown up in beautiful and useful ways to advance the work of nourishing cultures of leadership. They all contribute so beautifully to this work and to humanity.

Contents

Foreword 1

Preface 4

Introduction 9

Chapter One: The Blueprint for Optimal Health

Every Organism Has Within It the Blueprint for Its
   Own Optimal Health and Balance 18
Optimal Health Through Thoughts, Patterns of
   Information, and Perceptual Lenses 32

Chapter Two: Health and Balance for Optimal Effectiveness

Focusing on Genuine Contact Produces Tangible Results 44
Genuine Contact with Self 50
Establish a Foundation that Is Balanced 56
A Way of Increasing Your Genuine Contact with Yourself 76
Genuine Contact with Another 84
Judgment and Discernment 96
Genuine Contact with a Collective 104
Genuine Contact with Creation, with Creator, with Source 130

Chapter Three: Spirit Matters

Spirit or Conscious Energy Is All-That-Is 146
Theoretical Physics 156
Entrainment 164
Working with the Morphic Field, with Spirit,
　with Conscious Energy..174

Chapter Four: Change Is Constant

I Believe that Change with Its Accompanying Loss,
　Grief Work, and Conflict Is Constant..............................184
Organizations Thriving in Change 190

Chapter Five: Keep It Simple

I Believe In Keeping It Simple..210
Genuine Contact Tools and Frameworks............................216
Genuine Contact Processes 224
The Genuine Contact Organization 227

Moving Forward..232

Notes 234

With Gratitude...236

About the Author 240

Foreword

Not that long ago I had the most profound experience. I gifted myself with a four-day spiritual retreat—a time to be together with a group of people who I trust deeply to create a life-nurturing container for one another on our journey to live the full expression of our purpose on earth at this time.

As I traveled to the retreat, it was with a bit of trepidation. Up till now, when I've experienced deep processes like this, it has always come with much grief-work as I have unpeeled painful layers of my past and worked to understand myself more fully. Many a tear has been shed. That kind of work can often feel heavy and hard. I was committed, open to the experience, and yet not looking forward to it much.

As the days unfolded, I experienced lightness, peacefulness, calm, and joy. There was plenty of new awareness. New understandings of how I have been acting out my life and how I would like to show up going forward. It was truly a transformational journey. And not one tear was shed. Not a moment of grief. Instead, there was an ever-unfolding understanding of the beauty within my soul, a beauty that has been there all along and is ready to be expressed fully in the world. While the next steps on my path are clear, I am aware that there is much work to be done to get there, and it will be joyful and fulfilling work.

After talking with Birgitt upon returning home from this phenomenal experience, she reminded me that, although at 34 I am often still considered young by my peers, I have been on an intentional and committed journey in my personal development for nearly 20 years now.

Those 20 years illustrate how living and working the Genuine Contact way can look like. Being raised by Birgitt Williams and having had Ward Williams as a bonus-dad for nearly all of my adulthood has meant living in the immersion program of the Genuine Contact way, 24/7.

At its core essence, the Genuine Contact way of living and working is about being in genuine contact—with yourself, with one other, with the community, and with Creator. When applied to your life, it is about living the fullest expression of your divine beauty and inviting those around you to do the same. When applied to your work, the Genuine Contact way is about inviting everyone within the organization, whether one person or a thousand, to express their fullness in all that they do, to contribute to the collective wisdom of the organization, and to experience high enjoyment, high creativity, high productivity, and high engagement every day.

In my youth, as the Genuine Contact program was first coming into being, I was making my own commitment to myself to be in genuine contact, to live the Genuine Contact way. And the immersion experience began. I have been challenged to show up and be fully present in my life, to learn to speak my truth and trust that whatever happens is the only thing that could. To discover my purpose and passion in life and to pursue it fully. To lead my life from a place of clear and demonstrable values. To create a powerful vision for my life, set intentions, and then hold space to watch as the Universe has conspired to help them unfold. I am building a supportive and loving community around myself, and learning to ask for what I need and trust that my community will support me in realizing those needs. I am creating healthy and balanced structures in my life and in my work to support me in continuing to live the Genuine Contact way.

Foreword

Birgitt's writings in *The Genuine Contact Way* invite each of us to make our own personal commitments to ourselves. To commit to bringing the Genuine Contact way into our own lives and our organizations. The invitation is gentle. It is an invitation to take on what feels right for you at this time, and to set aside what doesn't resonate. It is an invitation to live a life that is fuller, richer, deeper, more conscious and more alive.

The Genuine Contact Way is the kind of book you can read now, and then read over and over again, taking your personal explorations deeper with each new experience. The invitation to connect to the Genuine Contact Way community invites you to be a part of something intentional, to connect with others who are also committing to themselves more fully. To support others and be supported as you explore your learnings. I look forward to meeting you there.

Rachel Amanda
Brantford, Ontario, Canada 2014

Preface

Be the Change That You Want to See in the World

Courageous living is what we are asked to embrace. As Mahatma Gandhi said, we must be the change we want to see in the world. It takes tremendous courage to be the change.

You are reading this book because you now want to embrace your courage and rise above your fear of achieving your fullest well-being, the well-being of any organization that you are in, including your family, and the well-being of humanity. In reading this book and participating in the Genuine Contact way of living and working to the extent that is right for you, you are committing to grow and expand to the fullness of who you are, learning to use your full potential.

This initiates change. Change takes us into the unknown. Do you recognize that you feel safer holding on to whatever you believe keeps you unhappy rather than facing the unknown? Change may result in gain and expansion, likely beyond what you envision. Change is also always accompanied by loss. I think knowing that change is always accompanied by loss is why people who would like to see their reality improved fail to take the necessary action. It is not resistance to change that tends to hold people in place; it is resistance to loss, ruin, and failure. This fear is a strong motivator. If you are like most people, you fear loss of job, relationships, familiar structures and beliefs, even loss of family. If you are like most people, you fear what is unknown because you fear loss, ruin, and failure. I assure you that the power within you individually and collectively is greater than the power of fear, and you will discover this when you embrace your courage to initiate changes in your life.

Humanity is at a crossroads: the direction we choose will affect countless generations to come. The choice is one of a life-nurturing future or a life-depleting future, of freedom or tyranny. I look into the eyes of my children, my bonus-children, and my grandchildren and I choose to do my part in creating a life-nurturing future. This eye contact, heart to heart, soul to soul, gives me courage. I choose to be the change that I want to see in the world and to undertake the internal work necessary so that I can be the change I want to see in the world. I understand that inner work is required to experience tangible results. I find that doing things in the external world to bring about change that is positive and life-nurturing takes courage, especially within family units and organizational units that are fraught with life-depleting patterns and habits. However, none of the external changes I took leadership in required the amount of courage that it has taken to do my internal change work. I am courageous. I greet you and honor you in embracing your courage too. Together we can choose a direction for humanity that will benefit countless generations to come, beginning with being the change we want to see in the world.

The good news is that there is nothing that we need to fix. Fixing something is about going backward and expending energy in ways that are probably not useful for the future. It is always good to learn from the past in terms of what worked and what did not work so that we do not repeat it. It is important to stay focused on solutions and not be dragged down by problems to "fix." If we focus on problems and fixing them, we are unlikely to achieve desirable life-nurturing results.

A solution is possible when we make more conscious choices toward the future we want to create. If we focus on what we want, in accordance with the Universal Law of Attraction, we will draw it into our reality. If we align ourselves with problems, we create problems. If we align ourselves with solutions that stem from being the change we want to see in the world, we contribute to creating them. We can hold visions of life-nurturing organizations that achieve extraordinary results for humanity and the planet, and we will contribute to their creation. We can hold visions of nurturing a culture of leadership in all organizations in which people thrive while achieving incredible results.

We can be the change we want to see in ourselves, our organizations, and our world … and then witness miraculous results.

As Einstein reportedly said, "We cannot solve our problems at the same level of thinking that we were in when we got into the problems." Sometimes this quote appears as "We cannot solve our problems at the same level of consciousness that we were in when we got into the problems." One way that I shift what might be perceived as levels of thinking is to shift *what* I choose to notice, what I focus on, and being willing to expand my perspective.

Now let us think about what it takes to shift to a different level of consciousness, if that is what Einstein was really advocating. It is helpful to shift from a linear perspective of levels of consciousness and replace this perspective with a picture of expanding consciousness, something all of us can choose to do as we lead our lives, our communities, and our organizations. It is also helpful to have a picture of multiple dimensions of consciousness, again knowing that each of us can access multiple dimensions of consciousness so that we can truly be in a different consciousness than we were in when we got ourselves individually and collectively into the problems we experience now.

Most people can easily access four dimensions of themselves, four dimensions of their consciousness. It takes only some simple work to get out of their mental consciousness, which is often dominant, and start paying attention to their physical, emotional, and spiritual consciousness. Each of these four dimensions of consciousness is a different dimension of the whole self that is already present. Yes, already present in each of us. Amazing solutions for our future can come out of shifting from one dimension of consciousness to working from the whole spectrum at once. Working from a greater spectrum of available consciousness shifts us from accepting that ordinary reality is the way life and leadership must be done. It shifts us to a life beyond ordinary reality, one that we might think of as an extraordinary reality. It is achievable.

Thank you for embracing the courage to create a life beyond the ordinary reality that we collectively experience. I encourage you to find the sources that will assist you in doing so. *The Genuine Contact Way* can be a resource for you in your journey. I am careful not to leave you with a message that there is only one way, as it is my desire to create an opportunity for you to empower yourself. If anyone tells you there is only one way, they are inviting you to give your power to their beliefs, giving up your personal power to lead your life that is your birthright in this freewill universe. In the pages that follow, I create the opportunity for you to use your courage to empower yourself and to find what works best for you in being the change you want to see in the world. Once you discover what is offered, it might feel right to align yourself with the vibrational field of the Genuine Contact way of living and working, as well as whatever other vibrational fields work to help you lead your life in the way you choose.

I offer you a perspective for changing your perceptual filters from your current view of ordinary reality to include what might now seem like non-ordinary reality. We can collectively make choices, one person at a time, to choose an extraordinary reality. Future generations may look back at us and acknowledge us for our contribution to shifting world consciousness. They might acknowledge our courage to make life-nurturing choices, choices of shifting our consciousness to achieve personal and organizational breakthroughs, to being the change we want to see in the world. They might look back at us and realize that we had the courage to shift from our current ordinary reality to what we currently perceive as non-ordinary or extraordinary reality. They will acknowledge us for our courage, for being willing to change, for being able to listen, and for getting out of our mental consciousness long enough to listen to the great wisdom of our spiritual, emotional, and physical consciousness. I intend that my grandchildren will be able to say, "Thank you for loving us sooooo much that you helped create a life-nurturing world for us."

Introduction

One day on a train ride when I was contemplating what my work in the world was to be called, I was inspired with the words "Genuine Contact." The inspiration took the form of a booming voice saying those words, interrupting my contemplation with an answer. I remember looking around at the other passengers in the crowded train to see if they were reacting as though they had also heard this voice. No one else seemed to have noticed, so I accepted that this was an experience that was for me and was divinely inspired. I thereafter dedicated my work to encouraging genuine contact in the world: genuine contact with self, with one other, with a collective, and with our Creator and creation.

One of my favorite concepts is "I wish each person could see themselves as the angels see them. They would know they are truly beautiful, gifted, powerful, and precious." I believe that it is important for people to claim the leadership of their lives, to claim their power, to take authority for their lives, to be accountable and responsible to themselves, and to expand themselves into their full potential. I believe people are precious.

When I live and work in my full potential, I experience a sense of order, design, expansion, balance, and harmony. I experience my life moving in a wonderful rhythm. I recognize that true wealth is spiritual, physical, emotional, and intellectual.

By profession, I am an organizational development consultant who specializes in developing leaders, developing organizations, and in assisting leaders and their organizations to find solutions in ways that are expansive and generate true wealth. As an organizational development consultant for over two decades, I have had the privilege of working with organizations of all kinds in many countries, assisting them in solving complex challenges to move themselves forward in meeting their goals. I have gathered a lot of data about what works and what does not work in organizations. I recognize that for organizations to experience breakthroughs to their true wealth, a shift in consciousness is needed. Fundamental to a shift in consciousness is nourishing a culture of leadership in our families and our organizations. This requires embracing a paradigm shift in how we regard leadership.

I wrote *The Genuine Contact Way* as a guidebook for people to learn to live and work from their full potential. It is constructed as a study book, with questions to be answered on your own or in study groups of two or more. Every segment offers concepts for your consideration. Every segment offers the opportunity for you to make a decision about how you intend to claim leadership of your life, leadership within your family, your community, and your workplace. You are offered the opportunity to think about your role in nourishing a culture of leadership wherever you find yourself.

As I wrote, I imagined that you would read a bit, pause to reflect and make notes for yourself, and develop agreements with yourself for leading your life based on what you felt was right for you. I have included pages within this book for taking these notes. I also imagined study groups in workplaces and other settings, studying the book together and using its concepts to improve their work and workplaces. There is a lot of potential to be tapped, and I imagined this guidebook assisting people, including leaders and their organizations, in making decisions to have a shift in consciousness to live their full potential, creating breakthroughs in their personal lives and

Introduction

in their organizations. I imagine that organizations everywhere can achieve their true wealth and fulfill their chosen purpose, vision, and goals. I imagine that through nourishing a culture of leadership in organizations, life-depleting choices will fade into the past and life-nurturing choices will be made benefiting people, society, and the environment for us and the generations that follow.

I am well aware that the written word might only leave you in your mental consciousness, unless I can somehow paint a word picture that engages your feelings. The reflection questions at the beginning of each chapter are intended to engage your emotional, spiritual, and physical consciousness, as are the questions that conclude each chapter. The choice to do this is, of course, yours, depending on what sort of experience you want at this time. I believe that the interactivity created by your reflections, your answers to the questions, and probing what is meaningful to you is where your learning will take place, not in my written words, which are intended simply to stimulate your responses.

The questions at the start of each segment are:

1. What color comes to mind?
2. What texture comes to mind?
3. What metaphor comes to mind?
4. What dance movement comes to mind?
5. What are you learning about genuine contact?

To deepen your learning experience from each segment, I have added four reflection questions at the end of each segment that are similar to questions considered in the practice of Neuro-Linguistic Programming (NLP).

The reflection questions are:

1. If what is conveyed here is true, what would I see?
2. If what is conveyed here is true, what would I hear?
3. If what is conveyed here is true, what would I feel?
4. If what is conveyed here is true, what would I know?
5. If what is conveyed here is true, how could this affect your leadership?

To assist your multidimensional learning, we have included a series of symbolic art images created by artist Laura Bolton specifically for those of you who learn best by looking at an image to provide impulses for reflection.

Connecting with the Worldview This Book Is Written From

Everything that you learn within *The Genuine Contact Way* is going to be understood from the perspective of your worldview. I think it is helpful to share my worldview with you so that you can determine the level of alignment that you feel, without having to guess throughout this book what worldview it is written from, and so you can make an informed choice of the level of involvement that you want to have with *The Genuine Contact Way*. When I read books or listen to someone, it assists with my engagement in the contribution being made if their worldview is explicit from the beginning. Maybe the same is true for you, and so I offer my worldview to you.

My worldview that has influenced the development of both the Genuine Contact way and the Genuine Contact program and the way I lead my life includes these five beliefs:

Introduction

1. I believe that every organism (including the organization) has within it the blueprint for its own optimal health and balance. I trust the people in the organization to know what is needed for optimal effectiveness. Building on the strengths within the organization is a key to optimal effectiveness. Sometimes individuals and organizations are toxic and because of toxicity cannot access their blueprint for their optimal health and balance. Toxicity is a barrier to optimal effectiveness that can be broken through when individuals and organizations attend to their balance, cleansing, and nourishing to nurture their life force.

2. I believe that focusing on genuine contact enables individuals and organizations to achieve the individual and organizational health and balance that is needed for optimal effectiveness. Positive change in the organization is directly linked to positive change in individuals. Both are required for sustainable new ways of working.

3. I believe that Spirit or spirit (conscious energy) matters; that, through spirit or Spirit, all of creation is connected; and that people are precious. My experience is that strategies based on these values have exciting, tangible results.

4. I believe that change with its accompanying loss, grief work, and conflict is constant. Individuals and organizations that develop mastery in working with change can sustain optimal effectiveness. These leaders and organizations recognize that change cannot be managed, that energy spent trying to manage change is wasted energy, and that productive use of individual and organizational energy is achieved by working with change rather than against it.

5. I believe in keeping it simple. Simple frameworks and processes enable success with complex situations. In keeping it simple, I recognize that any sustainable change must begin from the inside and cannot be externally initiated or driven.

It is up to you to decide how my expression of my beliefs that are part of my worldview feels to you. Perhaps by sharing my beliefs, I have gained or lost you as a reader of this book. Perhaps it is the worldview itself that causes you to engage or disengage your desire for learning from this book. Perhaps you choose to remain engaged with this book even though you disagree with the beliefs it is based on, and are simply curious about shifting consciousness to achieve organizational breakthroughs, particularly in shifting to a new paradigm regarding leadership. I am not asking you to agree with my beliefs, only to be informed that these are the beliefs that frame this unfolding story. If you are like me in this regard, you find it helpful to understand the underpinning beliefs from the beginning, removing the need for unnecessary guesswork and assumptions.

To explore the shift in consciousness that is necessary to shift to a new paradigm, this book has been structured in five sections in alignment with the five beliefs of my worldview. The new paradigm, if you choose to shift your consciousness individually and collectively, is one in which everyone is capable of leadership, leadership is a verb, and nourishing a culture of leadership is perceived as critical work for humanity to thrive for generations to come.

Introduction

CHAPTER ONE

The Blueprint for Optimal Health

I Believe that Every Organism (Including the Organization) Has Within It the Blueprint for Its Own Optimal Health and Balance

As you read this segment, to add experiences of your own, I invite you to reflect on

1. What color comes to mind?
2. What texture comes to mind?
3. What metaphor comes to mind?
4. What dance movement comes to mind?
5. What are you learning about genuine contact?

I believe that every organism, person, couple, family, team, and organization has within it the blueprint for its own optimal health and balance. I trust the people in every organization that I have ever worked with to know what is needed for optimal effectiveness. Conditions need to be created so that the wisdom inherent within the organism can be accessed and acted on. Louis Pasteur, on his deathbed, reportedly said, "I had it wrong. Don't go after the pathogens … go after the interior terrain." I agree with Pasteur.

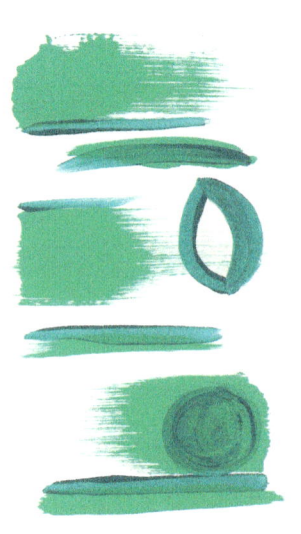

Attending to the "interior terrain" is about creating the right conditions so that the organism can access its own blueprint for its optimal health. Too often, "healing interventions," often quite well-intended, go after the symptoms while paying insufficient, if any, attention to the interior terrain, the conditions. For the physical body of the individual, there are many medical approaches that examine symptoms and singular systems and do not address the condition of the whole body. This is valuable in acute and trauma situations and far less valuable or effective in chronic conditions or general well-being. In chronic conditions and for general well-being, sustainably optimal results come from focusing on the health of the interior terrain.

Blueprint for Optimal Health of the Individual

I remember being diagnosed with arthritis at the age of thirty-one, being given the prescription medication that I was told I would have to take for life, and being sent on my way. This was an approach to my health focusing on the symptom. My inner wisdom, after a few days of taking the medication, caused me to pause and think. I realized that with every meeting I had during the day, and having a cup of coffee whenever a new person came into my office, I was having seventeen cups of coffee a day. I did not, at the time, understand about my interior terrain, and yet I realized I might be causing some of the condition I was in. I reduced my coffee intake to four cups a day, replaced the other cups of coffee with copious amounts of water, and stopped taking the arthritis medication. Within days, I no longer had pain in my joints and was definitely arthritis-free. The specialist had never paused to ask about my diet, about my interior terrain. I too had not paused soon enough to wonder about my interior terrain. I am grateful to that inner wisdom that caused me to pause, to examine, and to take action. I took only one simple step, which was to replace most of the coffee intake with water, and my body took care of restoring me to my optimal health at the time, quickly and sustainably.

Today, I seek out health practitioners who approach my health from a holistic perspective. I am not a symptom and I am not a system. I am interested in prevention more than interference. I am interested in working with health practitioners who assist me in doing what it takes to optimize my interior terrain so that my body can access its blueprint for its optimal health.

It takes courage for you, the individual, to admit that you have the blueprint for your optimal health and balance within you. It takes courage to admit that you, as a couple, have the blueprint for your optimal health and balance within you as a couple. It takes courage to admit that you as a family, a team, or any other type of organization have the blueprint for your optimal health and balance within your family, team, or organization. It takes courage, because up until now, you might have embraced the faulty thinking that has led you to believing in yourself as lesser than you are. As well as courage, it seems that some humility might be needed too; you have had the wisdom within you this whole time and have either not known about it or not used it.

Once I accessed the courage to accept the belief that within me is the blueprint for my optimal health, I have been able to stay in my optimal health most of the time and yet not all of the time. When toxins from my environment get the better of me, I too have to detoxify, cleanse, balance, and nourish myself to regain my optimal health. My experience is that because I believe that I have the blueprint for my optimal health within me, I return to my balance as an individual quickly. The same is true for me in all of my most precious one-to-one relationships and in my relationships with the organizations I participate in.

Chapter One: The Blueprint for Optimal Health

I struggled against this belief about the blueprint for my optimal health being within every organism for a long time, because if I accepted it, I would need to explore why my own health was not optimal, why I was heading for a divorce, why my family of origin had so many troubles, and why my childhood had such difficulties. It was much easier for me to stay plugged in to beliefs in which I was a victim of my circumstances and that my health, my marriage, and the baggage from my childhood was due to the behaviors of others, with my own role being quite small. I had quite a struggle with myself to come to terms with my own power, wisdom, and that the blueprint for my optimal health was within me, and the blueprint for the optimal health of any organization I chose to be in was also within the organization. I think the struggle was hard not only because of the need for courage and humility, but also because along with the belief came a lot of responsibility that I was not sure I wanted.

In my struggle to mobilize my own courage to accept this belief, I was grateful to my parents for their attitude about physical health, in which a doctor was rarely called in, and the use of pharmaceutical drugs aside from the occasional aspirin was not part of their lives. They believed in "letting nature take its course." In adulthood, when I was pregnant and giving birth to each of my four babies, the nurse practitioner who was the primary care person for me answered every question I had with "let nature take its course" and used a non-interventionist approach. Optimal health prevailed. And so I began thinking about the implication behind this phrase, which implies that optimal health will somehow show up if there is no intervention. Where does it show up from?

I read a lot in my search, and I observed a lot in my own life and in the lives of those around me. I came to understand that in the physical body, optimal health could not show up if there was a lot of toxicity. Along the way, recalling Pasteur's quote, "I had it wrong. Don't go after the pathogen, go after the interior terrain," I concluded that if the interior terrain was life-nurturing, pathogens would not hang around and optimal health would return. I found books on how I could detoxify my environment, eat foods that were healthier, exercise in ways that would remove toxins, and generally look after my interior terrain. In following the advice by author Andreas Moritz in his book *Timeless Secrets of Health and Rejuvenation*, I succeeded in creating the conditions in my body for the blueprint for my optimal physical health to be allowed to do what it does.[1] And yet, there are times when I would get sick or feel that I was not in my optimal health and balance, despite my care for my body. Sometimes I would get a cold or the flu. Sometimes I had aches and pains, the most severe of which were two dislocated kneecaps in the early days of a six-week trip to Russia and Germany. And then, of course, there was the frozen shoulder when I tore my rotator cuff. There is nothing that feels frozen about that condition. It is excruciatingly painful. If my blueprint for my optimal health was operating, how did I end up with setbacks? I continued to observe and to read.

It might have been obvious to me sooner, but it was not. Then suddenly, I understood that spiritual, mental, and emotional health and well-being affected physical health. Accessing the optimal blueprint for my perfect health was a multidimensional experience, including at a minimum the mental, spiritual, emotional, and physical dimensions. There were so many messages around me to guide me to this realization that it still baffles me how I ignored this conclusion for so long. This conclusion was even covered in some of the books I had read, and yet somehow I did not notice. What was I thinking? And yes, that is precisely the crux of the dilemma: *what was I thinking?* Where I chose to focus my thoughts seemed to be the key to accessing my blueprint for my optimal health and balance.

… Chapter One: The Blueprint for Optimal Health

I experimented and discovered that where I chose to focus my thoughts and accompanying words affected my physical health and my sense of optimal health and balance in all of my relationships. I concluded that the belief of the blueprint for optimal health being present for an individual also held true for all organisms, and that every organization was a living organism to which this applied—the couple, family, team, and even big global organizations. This conclusion might feel like a big stretch in the definition of organism. As an organizational consultant, I keep finding evidence that the blueprint for optimal health and the wisdom to get there is within the organization in one hundred percent of the organizations I have worked with. The wisdom sometimes fails to get acted on, but it is always there.

I have learned a lot about accessing the blueprint for my optimal health and learning to command the focus of my thoughts. It is an ongoing work in progress. Sometimes I have to marshal my thoughts while I am kicking and screaming, wanting to go the other way, because I lock onto previous thought patterns that are familiar and yet not useful to my well-being.

Blueprint for Optimal Health—Organizations

This blueprint for optimal health also applies to organizations. Over the past thirty-five years, I have worked with numerous organizations, including not only big organizations but also couples and families. Initially, when I am asked to be of assistance, I am asked to fix the symptoms, namely behaviors and actions that are seen as problematic and getting in the way of the organization functioning well. I had wonderful teachers who taught me not to get fooled by symptoms and to focus on the conditions within which those symptoms showed up. When I learned family counseling, I learned that when working with a family, there was often one child that the family would point to as the black sheep of the family, as the one causing the problems. It was like pointing out a symptom, and I was not to be fooled into pursuing the symptom. My job was to learn what the conditions were that caused the child to do this acting out.

I discovered that most of the time this child was the healthiest member of the family unit. The child still had the passion to act out, and in doing so, to seek help for a family that often was attempting to function in very toxic conditions. The interior terrain was so toxic, and this child was announcing it to the world with a plea for help. In those instances where the family worked at the conditions for the functioning of the family, the behaviors shifted when the conditions or interior terrain was developed to nurture life. The result of the "interior terrain" approach was sustainable in improved family life and improved child behavior.

I admire the work of the late Dr. Peter Frost of the University of British Columbia in Canada. He studied and wrote about a phenomenon in organizations that he referred to as the toxin handler. His well-researched thesis was that in toxic organizations, those that were not looking after the conditions of their organization, high-performing teams, if they could be found, were high performing at the expense of someone who was handling the toxic environment and keeping the toxicity away from the team. Imagine a cultural norm in which it is somehow acceptable to allow for toxic conditions for the workforce, within which it is expected that the head of the team must ensure a high-performing team with measurable goal-achieving results. Imagine that it is acceptable that this is at the expense of an individual who is a formal leader of the team or department—either the head of the team or the second in command.

Chapter One: The Blueprint for Optimal Health

Dr. Frost and his colleagues studied a sample of the people who were managing to achieve high-performing teams despite highly toxic conditions. They found that these "toxin handlers" handled the toxic environment and within the bigger toxic environment they created the conditions for their own team to have a nurturing environment. The result is the high-performing team. And the result is also that these toxin handlers actually pay with their own lives. They become ill, sometimes with heart attacks, sometimes with cancer, sometimes with other stress-related diseases.[2]

Dr. Frost and I talked about the high price of creating a life-nurturing environment in which the smaller organism (team) could function in a larger toxic organization, and neither of us thought it was worth this price. The better answer would be to create the conditions for the whole organization to be able to access the blueprint for its perfect health, and then every smaller organization inside the bigger one could achieve its optimal performance.

As an organizational consultant, I am only willing to work with leaders who are willing to address the interior terrain or conditions of their organizations. I find the results in such situations to be life-nurturing, sustainable, and achieve great results. I have no interest in wasting my time in putting my attention on fixing symptoms and thus achieving results that are not sustainable. To date, most leaders that have approached me have initially wanted a symptom to be fixed, a conflict to be resolved, or the behaviors and actions of a department to be corrected through better work processes. During the interview process, when I state my viewpoint regarding the ongoing conditions, which I refer to as the operating platform or foundation of the organization, rather than speaking to the symptoms of behaviors and actions, there are interesting responses. To date, eight out of ten leaders become clear that we are not the consultants for them. They want something fixed and do not want to address the conditions.

The good news is that two out of ten leaders are able to shift to extraordinary thinking, and they embrace the approach of addressing the interior terrain and accessing the wisdom of their people to figure out how to achieve optimal performance. Our role as an external consulting team then becomes one of working with the people, similar to the way that a midwife assists at a birth. We guide, counsel, mentor, reassure, provide simple tools and processes, and get out of the way so that the people inside the organization can access the wisdom within. One hundred percent of the organizations we have worked with have accessed the wisdom of the people, and the people have surprised their formal leaders with their solution focus for optimal performance. In addition, by involving the people in the organization in uncovering the solutions, there was no need to expend leadership energy to convince them to carry out the work to accomplish the solutions. Their commitment to action emerged while they were involved in figuring out the solutions. As an added bonus, the leaders who have been toxin handlers get a new lease on life when they no longer have to be the buffer between their people and the toxicity.

Many individuals and organizations are toxic, so you are not alone in coming to grips with whether you or your organization is healthy and balanced or whether you are at peak performance due to toxicity. Toxicity is a barrier to optimal effectiveness that can be broken through when individuals and organizations work to do so by attending to their balance, cleansing, and nourishing. This creates the conditions for life force to do its natural work. This is simply said and can be simply done as long as we do not resist the journey to our optimal health. For whatever reason, individuals tend to resist this journey, as do organizations.

Blueprint for Optimal Health ... My Relationship to Organizations

I have also learned that every organization that I might belong to is not for me to either continue being part of or to join, even though the blueprint for its optimal health is within the organization. Sometimes the nature of the organization is simply one that I am not in alignment with and I can feel that it isn't working for me. The organization itself is just fine. I don't judge it as good or bad. I simply did not have as good a fit with some, while I did with others. Yes, I went through with a divorce and a decade ago remarried. I did not fit well within the first marriage. I have found my true fit within my current marriage. Both marriages had a blueprint for optimal health, and yet the optimal health of the first could not get achieved, while the optimal health of my current marriage is present all of the time. I have participated in friendships, teams, and groups to which I never felt aligned, to others that I felt aligned to for a while, and to others that I always feel aligned to. In every case, the blueprint for optimal health existed, yet in some groupings was not accessed. Toxicity in organizations can be present, just as it is in the human body. Again, the pathway to detoxifying the interior terrain of the organization, just as for the individual, is related to what the thoughts and accompanying words focus on.

I am reminded of a story that my friend Debbie told me about giving up any negative talk for Lent. She would show up to the groups she belonged to, and when talk became negative about someone or something, she would not participate. She found that after two weeks, she was no longer invited to be in the group gatherings since she didn't fit. She was an individual who had the courage to choose health and balance, and the individuals who were aligned with the toxicity did not want her around. What would it have taken for the group to access its optimal health and balance? People who believe in the power of one would say that Debbie, using the full power of her leadership skills, could hold steady enough to create the shift for the whole group to align with her. People who believe in Critical Mass theory or the tipping point would say that once a percentage of the members of the group also decided to give up all negative talk, that a shift would happen in the whole group. Both of these approaches can take time. People who believe in miracles would say that a change such as complete detoxification could come about in an instant, possibly if two or more people desire an outcome for optimal health and balance of the group. There is evidence to support all these beliefs.

In this instance, Debbie did not pursue her desire for the group to access its blueprint for its optimal health, as it was easier to align herself with different groups and pull away from this one. We all make choices like that some of the time. In other groupings, such as that of a couple or of a family unit or an intact work team in which one might have a bigger investment, the choice is more likely to be different.

No matter the size or type of organization that you are a part of, if you believe that the blueprint for its optimal health exists and you wish to access it, you probably have some personal work to do. To some extent you, as well as everyone else involved, are likely keeping yourself, your marriage, your family, or your work team from accessing its optimal health. In order to do your part to access optimal health, you must desire it, mobilize your courage to allow yourself to change emotionally, spiritually, mentally and physically, and then get on with finding ways to detoxify yourself, nourish yourself, and create balance for yourself.

The key to this change seems to be getting command over your thoughts. There are many resources available to assist you in doing this. I know you will find the right one for you. I have come to conclusions for myself about thoughts. My thoughts go on ceaselessly. When I find them drifting to places that bring me to negativity, I can adjust the focus of my thoughts. Despite my desire to stay in only good-feeling thoughts, I get drawn back to thoughts that bring me to negativity unless I stay very focused on the types of thoughts I am having and redirect them when they start going where I do not want them to go. At first, doing this took a lot of energy. Now, "course correction" for my thoughts comes easier.

I have come to believe that thoughts gravitate toward patterns of information. The patterns of information that we have chosen to align ourselves with are the primary attractors for our current thoughts. If I have created an alignment with a pattern of information about something that I consider negative, my thoughts go to that pattern of information first. From this pattern of information, I construct and use a perceptual lens from which I see my world. Of course, I do not have only one lens going at a time. As a human, I am more complex than that.

Note to self: I choose to take command of my thoughts and to shift my thought patterns so that I do not allow myself to get trapped into a cage by my own mental focus.

Your turn

1. If what is conveyed here is true, what would I see?
2. If what is conveyed here is true, what would I hear?
3. If what is conveyed here is true, what would I feel?
4. If what is conveyed here is true, what would I know?
5. If what is conveyed here is true, how could this affect your leadership?

Notes

Optimal Health Through Thoughts, Patterns of Information, and Perceptual Lenses

As you read this segment, to add experiences of your own, I invite you to reflect on

1. What color comes to mind?
2. What texture comes to mind?
3. What metaphor comes to mind?
4. What dance movement comes to mind?
5. What are you learning about genuine contact?

As you read the following on thoughts, patterns of information, and perceptual lenses, please bear in mind that my journey in learning to command my thoughts was in order to align myself with beliefs that would allow me to access the blueprint for my optimal health as an individual and in all groupings that I am in.

When I wake up in the morning, I feel as if I am arriving in the new day, not sure where I am arriving from. I know I am arriving from sleep and dreamland, and I do not know where that is. When I wake up I take a quick check of my reality, starting with an external inventory. I feel comfort knowing that Ward is beside me, and when he is not there, I scan my mind to remember where he is. I become aware of the time and of the weather, and whether we are at home or in a hotel room. We have designed our bedroom to be like a hotel room, complete with an in-room coffee pot, because we spend so much time in hotel rooms that we jokingly thought this suited us.

My checklist then shifts to my internal inventory, starting with any immediate memories. It is at this moment that I sometimes remember that I have had a loss, or have been in disharmony with someone, have had a disappointment, or have had something that caused me to be sad or happy. In the actual moment of awakening, I have none of those feelings. It is during my checklist of arriving in my day that I remember the feelings I had on the previous day, linked to events in my life, and somehow I reconstitute those feelings and arrive right back into them, suddenly feeling sad or happy or disappointed despite the fact that no actual event in my new day created the feelings that I now experience.

At this point, my checklist has assisted me to arrive in my new day with data about my physical surroundings and data about the feelings that are the most recent ones I have had. I create some kind of linkage to the physical surroundings and to the emotions, like threads that anchor me into arriving in my day. I end up with physical symptoms of my feeling state, possibly a knot of anxiety in my stomach that hurts. I might discover that I have a self-critical voice that is the dominant voice in my head, assuring me that I have screwed up in something I have done or said, and my physical response is to cringe into an equivalent of a flight or paralysis mode. I might discover that I am feeling quite happy and peaceful with my world, and my physical response is a comfortable catlike stretch. The entire process of my checklist takes less than a portion of a minute. A lot has gone on in that short time, evoking thoughts, feelings, and physical states. This seems to happen on auto-play before I actually arrive in my day. In another instant, I realize that I have arrived in my day. Did nanoseconds pass? Did an eternity pass? So much happened that I am never sure. Both my physical and feeling states are the same as if I had just in this instant had a number of real and lived experiences. Yet I know that I did not. I am simply arriving in my awakened state, arriving in my day.

In that moment, I am aware that I am in a neutral, blissful state. I am conscious of it for that briefest moment. I believe that you also are in that state at that moment, no matter what is going on in your life. I invite you to be aware of this moment just before arriving in your day. What does your arriving process entail? Is it like mine? Do you sometimes discover the knots in your stomach, the sadness, the happiness, even though in the moment, no events have happened to bring you to that state?

I have come to recognize that what I am doing in that moment, before my momentum can start, is aligning myself with patterns of information that I access in my mind. These patterns of information, once accessed, involve my physical and emotional consciousnesses to such an extent that it is as if the event that originally elicited these responses has recurred.

Earlier in my life, I was unaware of this arriving process and simply got out of bed, bringing with me the results of the patterns of information I had aligned with, in an unconscious way. I dealt with all my life situations of the day from the perceptual lens created by my alignment with these patterns of information. I think you can imagine how I treated people when I was perceiving the events of the day from a perceptual lens in alignment with patterns of information that produced anger, sadness, or worry. This way of going into my day was not useful to me, to those around me, or to my work, and sometimes resulted in unnecessary difficulties for the people around me.

Today, I pause before getting out of bed and pay conscious attention to my arriving (into my day) internal process. I wish I could say that I can

Chapter One: The Blueprint for Optimal Health

retain the neutral, blissful state of sleep into my arriving into the day and throughout the day. I am not yet able to do that, although I am seeking it. I am still at the stage where I need to have a conscious process of commanding my thoughts to choose happiness, no matter what pattern my mind is attempting to align me with. By consciously choosing happiness, I am strengthening this pattern so that it always appears among my options in my arriving moment.

I can choose to align myself with the happiness pattern of information, and most mornings this is my choice. Within the reality of the patterns of information that I have access to, I have discovered that I can make conscious choices and that I can strengthen these pathways of conscious choices to become more and more automatic for me to align with. Now, in my arriving routine in the morning, no matter what patterns of information show up, I choose to be in a state of self-love, love for my fellow man, and to believe that all events of the day, no matter how they appear, are truly blessings as they appear in their various disguises. I think you can imagine how this might affect my perceptual lenses as I go about my day.

The start of my conscious awareness of this process began when I was learning from one of my favorite teachers, the late Dr. Angeles Arrien. She taught me that it was a good practice to pause before getting up in the morning to pay attention to whether I was in a state of self-love or self-critic. She guided me to stay in bed until the self-love was higher than self-critic, even if it was a ratio of 51 percent self-love and 49 percent self-critic. I started doing this, and discovered in the process that the self-critic voice, even so early in the morning, was often the stronger voice.

Accepting the teaching was the first step. Self-awareness was the second step, and in my case it was accompanied by a bit of shock that I had not known this about myself. As my next step, I took action by staying in bed in the morning, checking in with my self-love, self-critic quotient, and if the self-love was higher, I would bound out of bed very pleased with myself.

More often, the self-critic was the stronger, and the action I took was to lie in my bed, taking action to discipline my thoughts by using my imagination.

Imagination is a powerful tool. I imagined the love I felt for one of my babies, letting my mind drift back several years to the baby time. Once I locked on the feeling that I had had with my mind, I used my imagination to shift that feeling to my heart. Once the feeling was locked in my heart, I imagined that same feeling spreading throughout my body. Sometimes I could not achieve this total feeling of love, which started the self-critic all over again, because now I couldn't even get the remedial exercise right. I would take a deep breath and start over, commanding my thoughts to access the feeling of love and get it anchored through my body. Only then did I get out of bed, ready to engage in the events of my day with the perceptual filters that accompanied the state of love. I am of the belief that if I command my thoughts to align with the pattern of information of love or happiness, and I approach my life with this perceptual lens, I can approach any situation from a perspective that I will be happy.

I do not want to discourage you, yet I confess that the process of achieving this state in a consistent fashion for the majority of mornings took me several years. It was worth the effort, and may not take you nearly so long. My self-critic voice was a very loud one. When I didn't get to my morning state of self-love easily, my self-critic spoke up. When I left my bedroom and something occurred that frustrated me, my self-critic voice spoke up. When I struggled to silence my self-critic voice as I went through the day, the self-critic voice simply got louder, because now I was failing at staying in my chosen state of happiness. I think that in the new age belief process, this would be referred to as new age guilt. In the Christian perspective, this would be thought of as sin, not being able to love your neighbor as yourself. This could cause guilt. Guilt causes more self-criticism, not more love. Struggling seemed counterproductive, so I searched for what would work.

Chapter One: The Blueprint for Optimal Health

In searching, I concluded that every person on earth has addictions. There are substance addictions, with various techniques employed to overcome such addictions, including support groups and abstinence from the substance. I read that the most difficult substance addiction to overcome is the addiction to food, because a person cannot abstain from eating, as food is essential for survival. I thought about addictions that are not of a physical nature, but of an emotional, spiritual, or mental nature. I was addicted to the self-critic voice, and abstinence from the self-critic was not an option because my thought processes were always engaged. Likewise, I was addicted to worry. I watched others around me to determine if I thought they had addictions, and probably because I was looking for them, I saw addictions in everyone I looked at. Some people were addicted to the story of themselves as a victim, others were addicted to perfection, others were addicted to being or seeming to be busy and do busywork all the time, and others were addicted to worry and to stress.

At the point of this realization, I noticed, as though for the first time, a poster that I had up in my office that said, "Don't tell me to unwind; it is my stress that is holding me together." When I put it up, it was funny. Now, in my new awareness, it was not so funny anymore. I was announcing an addiction that I had. At about that time, my son Aaron told me that I worried needlessly about everything and that he would like it if I could stop worrying so much. Another one of my addictions, related to the one about stress, had been recognized.

It takes courage to become aware of something, not because it is difficult to face a truth, but because it heralds the need to make a choice. I could have chosen to be in denial about the implications of my new awareness, and yet now that I knew about my addictions, denial would not have been a comfortable place, and I would likely have added addictions such as alcohol or food or television to help me stay in denial. I could have made the choice to do something about my addictions, and this is the choice that I made, fueled by courage, recognizing that this choice meant I had to embrace change.

I chose to work on my addiction to worry. I purchased a roll of 50 pennies and placed them in a pocket of my jeans. Every time I noticed that my thoughts turned to worry, I moved a penny to the other front pocket of my jeans. Often I would move pennies 300 or 400 times a day. My self-critic voice broke in many times and I had to command it to be still and tell myself I was doing just fine. I did not struggle or allow a guilt trip. I chose to take on the belief that I could command my self-critic voice and it would obey. Every night, I posted the number of pennies I had moved and associated them with the amount of personal energy that I had used up in my addiction to worry, rather than it being available for creative purposes. I created a picture for myself of 1,000 units of potential creative energy for a day, and so when I used up 400 units in worry, I reduced my available creative energy to only 600 units, quite a drop from the 1,000.

After two weeks of this daily task, using the pennies to bring to my attention when my thoughts automatically drifted to worry, as though this was the default pattern of my thoughts, I discovered that I was moving less than 100 pennies per day. At the end of three weeks, I was moving less than 50 pennies per day. At about that time, my addiction to worry seemed to simply evaporate and has not returned in the decade since then. Yes, on occasion, when the event warrants it, I might worry about someone I love, or about leading a workshop the following day for which the sponsor created a last-minute change and our plans had to be revamped on the fly. I consider this type of worry normal, and it has a short duration. I no longer feel the pull of worry as something that I do whenever my mind is not occupied. This pattern of information has almost no pull on me. I do not say that it is not in the periphery of my mind. I simply say that its pull on my thoughts is

Chapter One: The Blueprint for Optimal Health

greatly reduced because I made a conscious choice to no longer align myself with this attractor field.

My addiction to worry was not the only pattern of information that was pulling at my thoughts with my willingness to go there. There were others that also kept me from accessing the blueprint to my optimal health, creating clutter and toxicity. Because I was now in more command of my thoughts, the work I did regarding worry had beneficial effects when I wanted to command my thoughts in positive directions no matter what pattern of information was pulling me.

It is my experience that I constantly align and realign myself with patterns of information throughout the day. I am grateful that I am more conscious of my process of doing so, and I'm aware that the patterns of information that I align myself with affect how I perceive events and people. In clearing up this toxicity in myself, I bring a cleaner me to all my relationships in all the organizations that I am in. I even feel that through focusing on commanding my thoughts for the purpose of accessing my optimal health and balance, I have shifted my consciousness to a more expansive state.

Note to self: I intend to shift my consciousness to a more expansive state by doing a daily check on whether I am bringing a clean me to all my relationships and the organizations that I am in. I intend to also be able to do this in my relationship with myself, which is the one that I have had the most difficulty with in the past.

I invite you to reflect on this chapter by discovering your answers to:

1. If what is conveyed here is true, what would I see?
2. If what is conveyed here is true, what would I hear?
3. If what is conveyed here is true, what would I feel?
4. If what is conveyed here is true, what would I know?
5. If what is conveyed here is true, how could this affect your leadership?

Notes

CHAPTER TWO

Health and Balance for Optimal Effectiveness

I Believe that Focusing on Genuine Contact Enables Individuals and Organizations to Achieve the Individual and Organizational Health and Balance that Is Needed for Optimal Effectiveness

As you read this segment, to add experiences of your own, I invite you to reflect on

1. What color comes to mind?
2. What texture comes to mind?
3. What metaphor comes to mind?
4. What dance movement comes to mind?
5. What are you learning about genuine contact?

Accessing the Joy of BE-ing

Many people today, for whatever reasons, stay in sustained states of flight, fight, or paralysis, all of which cause physiological responses. These are important for critical moments, but are impossible to sustain for long periods without losing genuine contact with the essential self. When we

Chapter Two: Health and Balance for Optimal Effectiveness

lose contact with our genuine self, we are only partially present, partially available, partially engaged. I have met so many people who are only partially engaged with life, and I have worked with so many organizations that cannot benefit fully from the people present because these individuals are only partially engaged with life. When genuine contact occurs, health and balance is achieved in both individuals and organizations. Positive sustainable change in organizations is directly linked to positive change in individuals. It is required at both levels for healthy, sustainable, and often innovative ways of working.

What is genuine contact? It is the process that helps us access true joy in relationship with one's self, at least one other person, with a collective, and with Creator (Source) and creation.

The Journey to 'I Know Who I Am'

Why are humans on a quest to know "Who am I?" In the Old Testament, Moses asks God who God is so that the prophet can tell his people who is promising to take them out of bondage in the land of Egypt. God's answer is, "I AM THAT I AM." I believe that at the end of our personal quests to know who we are, the basic answer will also be "I AM THAT I AM."

Why has it been so challenging for me to figure out who I am? In coaching thousands of people,

I realize that my quest is shared by many others. Some appear to reach the knowledge of who they are effortlessly, while others experience great struggle and pain in figuring out the answer to their quest. As I continue to move into the fullness of who I am, including my understanding of who I am, I learn more about genuine contact and how to be in genuine contact. The more I learn about being in genuine contact with myself and others and Creator, the more I have been able to stay in a state of joy. The more I am able to stay in a state of joy, the easier the journey has become.

Having looked deeply into the faces of my babies and grandchildren, it was obvious they were content just to be their most wonderful selves. I truly believe that babies are in genuine contact with Creator and creation. Perhaps they remember the joyous state of bliss their souls recently experienced in a sense of oneness with the Creator. Babies also seem to have no difficulty being in genuine contact with others, or with themselves. I do not know if they are in genuine contact with the collective of humanity on the planet, but I think this is true too. A baby seems to be in a natural state of peace or bliss. It is possible to startle a baby by blowing in the baby's face. When the startle response happens, it seems that the child's natural state of peace and bliss disappears for a time.

Over time, little children develop a "fight, flight, or paralysis" response in dangerous situations. If the situation is truly dangerous, this is necessary. These necessary responses in situations of danger become the "go-to responses" as the child grows into adulthood, with many life situations being perceived as dangerous whether they truly are or not. Many adults seem to stay stuck in flight, fight, or paralysis, forming barriers to the more natural state of peace and bliss. Rather than focusing on why adults get stuck in fear responses, it is more useful to focus on ways to move beyond the "go-to" fear response and find ways to again access joy. It is possible to move beyond the barriers and find ways to access joy by focusing on learning to be in genuine contact.

Chapter Two: Health and Balance for Optimal Effectiveness

During my own journey to know who I am, I found it helpful to recognize four different but connected circles of relationship. These include making genuine contact with myself, in one-to-one relationships, with a collective, and with Creator, whom I refer to as All-That-Is, Prime Creator, Source, and Mother/Father God. Following are insights I have gained that may be useful to you on your own journey.

Note to self: words are limiting, and so I choose to use the word Creator. Yet this word will not suit some people. I do not wish to get into religious concepts, as each person has their own faith. I know, however, that making genuine contact with this Higher Power is essential: perhaps I will find more ways to convey this principle that transcend religious traditions.

Your turn.

1. If what is conveyed here is true, what would I see?
2. If what is conveyed here is true, what would I hear?
3. If what is conveyed here is true, what would I feel?
4. If what is conveyed here is true, what would I know?
5. If what is conveyed here is true, how could this affect your leadership?

Notes

Genuine Contact with Self

As you read this segment, to add experiences of your own, I invite you to reflect on

1. What color comes to mind?
2. What texture comes to mind?
3. What metaphor comes to mind?
4. What dance movement comes to mind?
5. What are you learning about genuine contact?

Recognizing Your Worldview

Everything that you learn within the Genuine Contact way will be understood from the perspective of your worldview. As has been previously mentioned, we all have personal viewpoints, which affect how we take in information and how we share with others. Where did the deepest fabric of our beliefs come from? While I have worked with many people who have not taken either the time or the energy to examine their worldviews, I believe that it is vitally important to do so. Our beliefs are rooted in our worldviews, and if they determine what we want to manifest in our lives, we need to understand them.

In the book *The Seven Mysteries of Life*, there is a worldview postulated that mankind seeks to discover the answers to these seven mysteries, and that both science and religion attempt to provide answers.[3]

1. The abstract nature of the Universe
2. The interrelatedness of all creatures
3. The omnipresence of life
4. The polarity principle
5. Transcendence
6. The germination of worlds
7. Divinity

This is one example of a worldview from which beliefs, assumptions, behaviors and actions have developed.

In various books, including *The Message of the Divine Iliad*, the late American scientist and philosopher Dr. Walter Russell shares stories that emerge from his worldview about all power coming from ONE, getting engaged, and ultimately returning to the ONE, with recognition that the world is in motion.[4]

Again, this worldview, shared by the followers of Dr. Russell, resulted in beliefs, assumptions, and behaviors and actions.

Christians, Jews, and Muslims define their worldview by affirming that in the beginning was the Word, and the Word was from the ONE, and then motion happened.

New Age thinkers describe their worldview as consisting of massive waves of light coming into our dimension now. They assert that all of humanity is beginning to feel the impact that we are, indeed, connected to all life. What affects one, affects everyone.

I believe that all of this remains a mystery. Yet, within this mystery, each of us has adopted or created a worldview from which our own beliefs, assumptions, behaviors and actions emerge. Whether or not you are religious, your worldview has been influenced by religion. It seems that when enough people agree on a set of rules that make up the pattern of information of a worldview, a consensus reality gets formed, to which others might or might not be attracted.

I think it is helpful to share my worldview with you so that you can determine for yourself the level of alignment that you feel, without having to guess what worldview the book is written from. This way you can make an informed choice of the level of involvement that you want to have with the Genuine Contact way, as the Genuine Contact way is influenced by my worldview. Every one of us views the world through our own filters. In my commitment to integrity, I feel that it is imperative to share the filters that I am writing through. I do not want to manipulate anyone by having a subtheme created by my worldview that is not transparent. I believe that such transparency is linked to operating with integrity. I can only speak about those filters created by my worldview that are in my conscious awareness and apologize if there are other filters that you pick up that may be outside of my conscious awareness, in the realm of beliefs, driven by what has been termed the subconscious. What a powerful processor that subconscious is!

The following are aspects of my personal worldview at this time:
- Humanity would be more consciously evolved if spirituality had not been separated from science.
- Life is enhanced when we work from physical, emotional, mental, and spiritual consciousness, allowing for evidence from the data of the physical and also evidence obtained through thought, feelings, intuition and deep knowing, even if it cannot be measured.

- All religions work to explain life and have a great deal in common with each other when they are collapsed to their basic beliefs. The Christian perspective is the one that I know the best, and despite embracing many other religions and belief systems, my worldview is most informed by the Christian worldview at its most basic in the actual writing and sayings of Jesus, who taught about love.
- Science works to explain life and science is running on a parallel track to religion in this regard, without science being able to explain religion or vice versa.
- Successful evolution of our organizations and humanity is dependent on the inner evolution of the individuals involved.

It is up to you to decide how my expression of these aspects of my worldview feels to you.

Note to self: this section on aspects of my worldview feels so important to share, and yet it has been awkward to write. I wonder if I am simply stating something which is obvious to people and doesn't need to be said.

Your turn.

1. If what is conveyed here is true, what would I see?
2. If what is conveyed here is true, what would I hear?
3. If what is conveyed here is true, what would I feel?
4. If what is conveyed here is true, what would I know?
5. If what is conveyed here is true, how could this affect your leadership?

Notes

Establish a Foundation that Is Balanced

As you read this segment, to add experiences of your own, I invite you to reflect on

1. What color comes to mind?
2. What texture comes to mind?
3. What metaphor comes to mind?
4. What dance movement comes to mind?
5. What are you learning about genuine contact?

The late Dr. Angeles Arrien in her work *The Four-Fold Way* of indigenous peoples on the planet, provides a simple assessment tool for determining if you are in what she calls right relation with yourself. In your journey of making genuine contact with yourself, answering these questions is a good and easily accessible starting point. She asks four questions:

1. When in your life did you stop dancing?
2. When in your life did you stop singing?
3. When in your life did you stop loving the telling of and listening to story?
4. When in your life did you start to fear the silence?[5]

Chapter Two: Health and Balance for Optimal Effectiveness

I had said that these questions were simple, making it easy to begin to access your state of genuine contact with yourself. You probably found them simple and profound. I personally find that it is the simple questions that are more profound than the complex ones, not because of the question, but because of the depth of the answer that they can generate. These profound questions create a great entry point into the journey of achieving genuine contact with yourself.

When I first heard them, I certainly paused to take stock of my life at the time. I found that I hadn't stopped dancing. That was good news to me. Some years later when I met Ward and he told me that he hoped it was okay that he didn't dance, I took a deep breath. How would I manage to keep dancing if my life partner did not dance? Would I give up an aspect of myself that the dancing represented? I needn't have panicked. It turned out that despite few previous occasions to dance, he did just fine and his love for me brought him to dance with me. Today, when doing our Y-Dan's (a form of tai chi) in the morning, we turn the last few poses into dance steps with each other, and I get such pleasure that my husband, who said he did not dance, actually dances with me every morning. So, I am fine with the dancing part of me.

I stopped singing when I was about twelve and was looking at my kindergarten report card. I loved school and loved my kindergarten teacher. She had written in my kindergarten report card that I loved to sing and it was just too bad that I was always out of tune. When I was in kindergarten, I had thought she complimented me when she said I loved to sing. At twelve, I realized I was not being complimented. This might not seem to be such a big statement, and if I had been more in touch with myself, it would not have deterred me. However, at the time I was a shy preteen without sufficient self-esteem, and so I simply stopped singing. This phase of me abandoning part of myself lasted about a decade, and then with the birth of my babies, I found my voice again to sing the lullabies that were needed to sing them to sleep. Doug (my first husband) played his guitar and we sang … we did a lot of singing. So, I am fine with the singing part of me.

I have never stopped loving story, the reading and the telling of stories. I have been an avid reader throughout my life. I have realized that the stories in the books I read had a lot to do with keeping me sane through some very difficult periods. I could be very upset, and by reading a story, I could go into the story emotionally and have my emotions calmed and balanced in the process. I found story to be exceptionally healing in my life journey.

The big one for me was the idea of loving silence. The question about when did I stop loving silence was posed to me when I was thirty-seven. I shuddered to think that someone could love silence. Beginning as a young child and for the balance of my relationship with my mother, silence was used as an effective punishment tool. I would discover myself in situations where the punishment was one day, or even five days, of silence. The longest duration was two years. I definitely did not love silence and perceived any silent moments as a punishment. This resulted in me carrying out a lot of my teenage years very actively with friends, sometimes creating so much activity around me that it was almost as busy as a constant party. This level of activity carried on as an adult, with my family, my friends, and my work. The question about when did I stop loving silence really jarred me. I must have been ready to listen to the question, because I paid attention when I heard it. I might have been able to hear it out of my respect for Angeles Arrien, or because I was ready to hear it in my quest for genuine contact with myself, or likely a combination of the two. I wondered what all of the developed and undeveloped aspects of me were that were tied into my fear of silence. I very much

Chapter Two: Health and Balance for Optimal Effectiveness

wanted to be whole and decided that I would figure out how to start loving silence.

I am not a person who does things partway. I made arrangements for time off of work, arranged child care for my children, and put everything else in my life on hold. I signed up for what is called a silent retreat offered by the Jesuits in a nearby town at their facility. There were options. I signed up for seven days of silence. I was allowed to bring books and audiotapes. No television, no phone, and no communication even with the Jesuits who were present, with the exception of a fifteen-minute guidance session with a spiritual director every morning. The first few days were almost too difficult for me to handle. I walked a lot, staying as physically active as I could to stave off the rising panic. On the third day, when I woke in the morning, there were tears on my face and I felt such a beautiful sense of peace ... with the silence. To this day, I am deeply grateful to the Jesuits for offering this opportunity to people for their healing. I came to understand what a great gift this was. As I went on in my life following that week, I have continued to embrace silence as a profound and wonderful aspect of life. In my work as an organizational consultant, I make frequent use of silence as an effective tool for people to achieve their learning and solutions. Because silence is not commonly used as a tool in organizations for getting business done, and because I assume that any group has people in it who have not yet learned to love silence, I always precede these times of silence with "if no one is saying anything and there is silence, it is not intended to be uncomfortable silence ... it is simply the silence that we need to gather our thoughts."

I provided these four questions for you because they were very helpful to me. Answering these four questions provided a base that kept me in sufficient balance to accelerate my journey of being in genuine contact with myself. Through answering the questions and establishing a sense of balance for myself, I was able to understand the importance of a solid foundation from which to do my conscious change work that would allow me to be in genuine contact with myself. A foundation that provides balance is a key ingredient for increasing the capacity for genuine contact, from my perspective. It does not matter how you get that balanced foundation. This was something that worked for me. In fact, until I had answered the four questions, I did not understand that I was not in genuine contact with myself, nor had I understood that I had avoided this part of my journey because I did not have a balanced base to undertake the journey from. A physical foundation is needed in order to do what can be called spiritual work, because without the foundation, the spiritual work will likely crumble around you.

I was in a state for much of my life of "I don't know what I don't know," and so after answering these questions, I ended up in a state of "Now I know what I don't know, and I don't know who I am." I had awoken to this fact from a life that appeared full and yet within which I had been avoiding myself. At thirty-eight and as a wife, a mother, and a CEO of a nonprofit organization, I had this awakening of realizing I did not know myself. From the outside, I probably looked as though I was much more self-assured and self-aware than I was. I was seen to be successful. In my years as a consultant, I have spoken with countless executives who are in their fifties and sixties and deeply frustrated because they do not know who they are, and had gotten to the stage of life where the compromises that they had made to be a role rather than a person were no longer tolerable to them. In hindsight, I am happy that I discovered this when I was thirty-eight.

With the concepts that I now have, I can tell you a little of what happened that took me to being thirty-eight without being in genuine contact with myself. I believe I began life in genuine contact with myself. Somehow, this sense disappeared. I am not sure of all the circumstances

Chapter Two: Health and Balance for Optimal Effectiveness

and think that it is not important to share what I do know. At the age of six, I simply went into hiding from myself. I do not think that my story is so special. It is simply a story. Everyone I have talked with has their own story of when and how they stopped being in genuine contact with themselves. Psychiatrists might say that these stories are related to our ego development. I don't know if they are completely right. I think there is much more of our whole self involved than just the ego.

I think that when we stop being in genuine contact with ourselves, we give up our sense of personal power, and in doing so, we develop addictions. In some people, these show up as substance addictions, and in other people they show up as mental or emotional addictions, such as addiction to worry, addiction to perfection, addiction to hiding and deception, addiction to the need to know, and so on, that seem to grow stronger over the years. My particular addictions showed up primarily in worry. I turned to alcohol at sixteen, but fortunately by eighteen ended that means of escape before it became an addiction.

Another key ingredient to accelerating a journey to being in genuine contact seems to be some sort of crisis. For me, the crisis was that my marriage was coming apart. I made a decision to do what I needed to develop myself further so that whatever part I was playing in our situation could be changed. I took a few workshops, the most significant of which were Process Theology with John Cobb, Process Facilitation with Marge Denis, Open Space Technology with Harrison Owen, and the Four-Fold Way with Angeles Arrien. The combination of the learning and my commitment to answering my quest of who I was gave me a giant leap in figuring that out. Rather than bringing my ex-husband and me closer together, my development took us further apart. The marriage ended and I began a time as a single mom of four children, who had visits with their dad. It was a difficult time, and yet I was in a new stage of genuine contact with myself. I continued my commitment to my growth, feeling as though my life depended on it. Along the way, in my relationship work, I made some choices that I would say were poor choices, except that they ended up being blessings because they are part of the story of how I became genuine with myself.

With personal drama going on, four children to do right by, and an organization to lead, I developed some health issues and had a personal crash, landing in what some people and poets refer to as the dark night of the soul. I woke one morning and could not stop crying. I discovered that I was unable to tie my shoes or do up my buttons, yet I had a presentation to give at the Chamber of Commerce. Somehow, I made breakfast for five of us, made four lunches, got the children off to school, and out the door I went, miraculously driving myself into the city, and made the presentation. That ended up being my last day of work for two months. The doctor diagnosed me with depression and prescribed a common and multi-side-effect antidepressant drug, which I subsequently took myself off of. Taking myself off the drug felt worse than the actual collapse. Friends said I was experiencing the dark night of the soul. My inner experience was that my soul was doing just fine and was in fact the reason that I made it through this period. I was having a dark night of the ego, as I was finding my new perception of myself in somewhat of a collision course between how I was leading my life based on my previous perception of myself and my true self. I discovered that I had allowed multiple compromises of myself in relation to who I really was. I had now reached another level of genuine contact with myself. I don't recommend this approach, and yet I see something like this happening all around me with those who have been labeled with "depression."

When I arose from that challenge into the more complete me through improved genuine contact with myself, I altered some of my patterns. In the process I lost some friends. Every stage of my growth has included losing some friends. A close girlfriend said, "I see you going through a door and I am not willing to follow." I give her credit for recognizing I was going through a door in my growth, and that for reasons of her own, she did not want to allow herself to grow at that time. The reason I give her credit is that, although she was afraid that our friendship might not make it, she neither stopped me from going through the door nor seemed to judge me. In so many situations, I have witnessed people undergoing the difficult lessons of their growth, only to have their friends pull them back. This is like the story of the crabs being harvested and put into baskets, and some crabs are trying to get out, and their buddies in the basket pull them back in for their own false sense of security. Years later, this girlfriend went through the same kind of door to her genuine self.

I wish I could reassure you that getting into genuine contact with yourself does not result in loss, yet I cannot give that reassurance. There is always loss when getting into genuine contact, first and foremost with a definite loss of previous dearly held patterns of thinking and behavior. As humans, we tend to lock onto certain patterns of information and lock out others that are right in front of us. When we grow, this firmly held "locking on" is disrupted, and it is actually useful to lose it. If the people around you are also committed to their growth, you might not lose them, because their own awareness of losing previously locked-onto patterns is expanding too. There is no certainty that you would have losses of the magnitude that I did—of marriage, of ego, and of friends. Yet, I cannot assure you that this will not happen.

This probably causes you to wonder why you would even consider working at being in genuine contact. As I have mentioned, I think the fear of loss is what holds most people back from being in genuine contact with themselves. It is quite a position to be in. If you override your fear of loss and get on with figuring out how to be in genuine contact with yourself, you will end up with some loss in your life, possibly some significant losses. You also might end up with a lot to gain, including a real sense of who you are, why you are here, and that you are powerful beyond what you currently understand yourself to be in creating the life you want.

I look at that same predicament and accept that it was what I went through with both the loss and the incredible gain. The former was exceptionally painful. The latter continues to be exceptionally wondrous. I also imagine having a door in front of me to my growth in my genuine contact. Not going through that door just so that I could control my growth and keep things the same would have reduced the potential for loss—but it would have also held me back. I think if I had done this, I would not have been able to bear myself and would have paid a different price, probably through a form of disease. As I understand it, physical disease is a manifestation of spiritual and emotional dis-ease or dis-harmony. *"It is more important to know what sort of person has a disease than to know what sort of disease a person has."*—Hippocrates (460–377 BC)

In advising my children, my bonus-children, and their partners about a path to take, I strongly advise them to take the risks involved in being in genuine contact with themselves and then seeing where everything else lands. It is my hope that my grandchildren will not need to go through this struggle and that they will not lose their current ability to be in genuine contact with themselves. We have it within us as a family to create the conditions for them to be nurtured for exactly who they are and never to lose their ability to lead their lives. I very much like that this family is conscious of the importance of this in the way that we have come together to support this new generation of precious beings.

Take Some Simple Baby Steps

I would like to share some insights with you that might be useful as you work to be in genuine contact with yourself. Use what is useful and ignore the rest. Each of us is unique, with our own way of doing things. First, it is helpful to realize that you give something too much power by being afraid of it. Your personal power ends where your fear begins. What fear are you giving your power to in relation to being in genuine contact with yourself? Oh yes, being in genuine contact with yourself is about claiming your full power and moving beyond fear. It is then up to you to figure out whether you want to use this power wisely and well.

To be in genuine contact with yourself, you need to get out of your head and into your heart, gut, and body. You might be surprised to discover that there is a lot more to you than you had previously thought there might be. You will discover that you are a multidimensional being and that you can expand your awareness far beyond what you are currently allowing yourself to be aware of. You have physical, mental, emotional, and spiritual consciousness, and you are able to listen to and understand these four dimensions of yourself. Yes, you can tune in to your four streams of consciousness, your four intelligences, to increase your experience of your genuine contact with yourself. This expansion of your perceptual filters from one dimension to four dimensions is a beginning and can be achieved with baby steps.

I have expanded my consciousness to these four dimensions by taking on assignments for noticing things. Yes, the baby step to take you to genuine contact with four dimensions of yourself is to actively notice things. I hope this does not seem too simple to you and that it feels like something you can do, even if only to see if it works in the way I have told you. At the start of each chapter of this book, you are asked to notice things from all four dimensions of consciousness as you go through the chapter. When you read a chapter in this way, you engage more of your whole self. At the end of every chapter, there are additional questions. They invite you to reflect on what you have noticed, again involving all four dimensions of your consciousness. This is modeling to you that it really takes very little extra time to expand your awareness using more of your multidimensional whole self. There is the time you took to read, and a little extra time, but only a little, to pay attention differently.

Noticing as an Exercise

Notice what you notice. What is interesting to you in the moment? As you are noticing from your expanded awareness, play with what comes up for you, and you will achieve even more genuine contact with your whole self.

A key to being in genuine contact with yourself is to shift your consciousness to notice things more, to notice what is happening around you. You end up getting in touch with how limiting your ordinary perceptual filters are, and how much better it feels to allow yourself to be in your non-ordinary reality of an expanded viewpoint. This non-ordinary reality is very much part of you that you don't usually recognize. There are different spiritual practices within which there is a stage of the student being set the task of sitting quietly and writing down everything that she notices, in the same spot, day after day.[6] At first, this can seem boring. Yet, as the days progress, she discovers that from the same seat, there is more and more to notice. The ordinary reality around her isn't what changes. There is something inside her that changes from the exercise of noticing. Initially, she notices from the perceptual filter that she usually applies to how she observes life. As she carries out her task, day after day, she notices more and more because she starts to observe the same reality from additional perceptual filters that allow her to notice things she never noticed before. She now notices from her non-ordinary reality, making greater genuine contact with herself. As the late Dr. R. D. Laing noted:

> The range of what we see and do is limited by what we fail to notice.
> And because we fail to notice that we fail to notice,
> There is little we can do to change. Until we notice.
> How failing to notice shapes our thoughts and deeds.[7]

I invite you to follow me as I take on a simple exercise to expand my awareness in noticing. Every time I do an exercise in noticing, my conscious awareness of my expanded self increases and never returns to quite the same "me" that I was when I started the exercise. I love the adventure of knowing that even though I am in genuine contact with myself, there is more of me to make genuine contact with.

Starting point: I pay very little attention to textures when I observe things.

Desired outcome: taking my observation of texture out of my non-ordinary reality and into my ordinary reality.

During the writing of this book, I was guided to explore clothing in a thrift shop and to pay attention to the textures of the fabric I encountered. The idea had two purposes, which were interwoven. One was to create an assignment for me to stimulate my creativity for the book content, with a goal of weaving the feeling of textures into the story. The second was to create the conditions within which I would have an opportunity to have a big "aha" that would stimulate my ability to convey the textures in the writing. I told Ward of my assignment and asked him to drive me, because I assumed that I would get so wrapped up in the world of textures and expanding my awareness that I would not be in the best condition to drive home after the experience. We created a date that included a stop at the thrift shop followed by a romantic supper out.

The shop we chose was Cause for Paws, which sold items to raise money for saving the lives of animals. That felt just right to me. I had never been there before, so my decision to go was not based on ordinary reality data; it was based on my inner knowing. I giggled as we set off, because I was approaching this shopping trip differently than any other shopping trip I had been on, and it felt like a grand adventure. I love the childlike curiosity that I feel when I do something I have never done before. I had been shopping in thrift shops many times before with the perceptual filter of noticing items in my size that attracted me that I might purchase, and being drawn to items by colors that appealed to me. It was my ordinary perceptual filter for a shopping trip, with colors giving me joy. Today's trip to the thrift store required me to shift my perceptual filter to the non-ordinary, and I discovered that childlike joy welled up in me as a result. I was to explore the clothing, not from the perspective of making a purchase, but from the perceptual filter of noticing textures in relation to possible benefit for the unfolding story in the book. Such a simple shift from my ordinary perception to my non-ordinary perception took me into the joy of childlike curiosity.

Chapter Two: Health and Balance for Optimal Effectiveness

Upon arrival in the thrift shop, the clerk greeted us warmly with a hearty "Welcome to Cause for Paws." I appreciated the warmth of the greeting, which I noticed she gave to every customer who entered. I also had a momentary feeling of guilt, knowing that she assumed I had come in to shop. I took out my writing pad, took a deep breath, remembered my commitment to my guidance to use a different lens to view the clothing than my normal shopping one, and established in my own mind that I was here to explore textures. Having established the rules for my adventure, I noticed that none of the clerks approached me, interfered with me, or asked me what I was doing. Rather, they carried on with their business as though I was invisible. I liked the freedom of how I was feeling to have my uninterrupted adventure.

Immediately, bright white catches my eye. I think of purity and the beauty of the white, and then remember that the perceptual filter is not color but texture. I take another peek at the white and then notice that one of the shirts has delicate sunshine-yellow flowers. I love the contrast and sigh, realizing that I wish that the assignment was about colors, which is a perceptual lens I love getting absorbed in.

Sparkly sequins catch my eye, on a brown fabric. The sequins are beautiful. The texture of hard plastic isn't pleasing to me, and suddenly the beauty fades and the hardness of the plastic looms larger in my view. As this adjustment occurs from the perceptual lens of color to the perceptual lens of texture, the same reality suddenly looks different, almost as though a light has been switched on to illuminate what is really there. The brown material that the sequins are on is soft and 100 percent cotton, vibrating authenticity, and I like that. In looking at the tag as I was feeling the material, I also noticed the words *Self Esteem USA, made in India* and I laughed at the message of the self-esteem of the USA being made in India. I also made a new rule about my adventure. I could notice colors and tags as well as textures, and I would still be on my assignment, so long as my primary perceptual filter was for the textures. If I was going to get lost in a perceptual reality during the adventure, the *getting lost in textures* was acceptable, while *getting lost in tags and colors* would not be acceptable.

The burgundy sparkly fabric was next, with its brushed look, giving it the appearance of great softness. I rubbed it with my fingers, only to discover the texture was scratchy and not soft at all. I created an assumption from this experience that looks can be deceiving. Just as I was writing my assumption down, I heard the clerk saying to someone, "That's the mystery," while laughing. Now I knew she must be talking to someone else, but in that moment, I felt she just might be talking to me. So I related my conclusion about how sometimes looks can be deceiving to what I was supposed to understand about the mystery. I looked over my shoulder to see if by chance the clerk was an angel in disguise and was indeed speaking to me about the mystery. But no, she was over at the cash register having a conversation that I could not hear. It is interesting how only this one sentence had jumped out, as though spoken right to me. I made a note of what I had noticed and then made another note about life wisdom, reminding myself that things that look cuddly, soft, and inviting might end up being scratchy. My mind immediately went to someone I once knew who could fit that description. That is another story. My quick peek at the tag brought giggles as I read "Divine USA." I was beginning to wonder if the words in these tags were jumping into my reality or if these were truly the tags.

A tank top of bright red and yellow caught my eye. Try as I might, I could not stay with the perceptual filter of texture and got lost in the colors again. The bright red front was lined with black. The bright yellow back was lined with purple. It was reversible and looked like it might be for a clown. I loved it and immediately decided that I wanted to create a dress-up box for my grandchildren and that this would be the first purchase for the box. I could imagine very kinesthetic Jessica putting this on, parading around, and reversing it while in motion, changing the colors and laughing. I could

Chapter Two: Health and Balance for Optimal Effectiveness

then imagine Marleigh savoring the silkiness of it and wearing it like a princess dress at a tea party. And with this thought process, I laughed.

I had jumped perceptual filters, going to my ordinary reality ones of shopping and colors, and only when I thought of Marleigh and her love of textures did I remember that I was to have my *noticing textures* focus on. I found it decidedly difficult to shift from the ordinary perceptual filter to the non-ordinary one and to stay in the non-ordinary one even when having fun. I could only imagine my straying back to my ordinary perceptual filter when I am asked to examine something more serious and not as playful as this *texture* exercise. As I stood there and thought about it, I wondered if approaching serious subjects playfully would be possible for me and if this approach would even be helpful. I find it difficult to imagine that I can access the playful part of my nature that frequently or for a sustained period, especially when I am feeling stressed.

I continued my exploration, attracted to a pale gray tank top that had pale blue lettering saying "Mudd Jeans" with a little handprint in the same color. I laugh. For me, mud = play, with memories of my children when they were young making mud pies and lying down in mud puddles to make the mud equivalent of snow angels. The shirt elicits fond memories of playing with my children. I again am not focusing with my perceptual lens about *texture*. And then I laugh, realizing that the theme of *play* has surfaced again. I reminded myself to explore the texture and loved the softness of the pure cotton. I could imagine how soft it would be to wear. And then I immediately shut down the perceptual filter of *shopping* before I again deviated from my assignment. The song playing in the store catches my attention, with the lyrics coming as though right at me: "Don't do it." I laugh. Why would those lyrics suddenly come to my attention when I had earlier simply assigned the store music a back seat in my attention so that I could pay attention to *textures?* This was just like the experience of suddenly hearing only one sentence from the sales clerks' conversation. Was this by chance a side effect of shifting my focus from my ordinary reality to my non-ordinary reality? Was my overall field of noticing expanding?

I took a deep breath to focus myself on keeping my perception on *textures*. I increased my focus on *textures* for the balance of my time in the store. I noticed materials that looked like silk but felt harsh, and others that looked like silk and felt so smooth. There were materials that had some parts of the pattern raised higher than others that made playing with the patterns fun as my fingers identified two textures, contrasted even more by one being brushed and the other being smooth, and I was mesmerized by the feel of lace that allowed me to poke my fingers through it and really play with scrunching it up into different configurations.

I would like to say that I was able to stay with my non-ordinary perceptual filter of *texture* and stay true to my task. I simply could not do it. Yes, I had a focus on texture, but I struggled to keep it as my primary focus. My ordinary perceptual filters continued to override the non-ordinary one. I found five items to purchase, including three for my grandchildren's dress-up box and two for me. Ward laughed when he saw me heading to the cash register, knowing that this was not my assignment. My bigger challenge was keeping my ordinary perceptual filter regarding colors and my very usual pattern of being drawn into colors in the back seat, allowing the non-ordinary perceptual filter of *texture* to be the dominant one. Colors won more than did texture. I decided to be pleased with myself that texture was dominant at least some of the time.

As I thought about my struggle to stay focused on textures, I realized that I had not been guided to ignore other aspects of the shop's clothing. I was not obligated to abandon my old filters. If I stopped struggling with myself, I could maintain my ordinary awareness of color and purchasing, and add the previously less-appreciated awareness of texture. In fact, I had begun to pay more attention to reading the information on labels as well. Through this very simple exploration of noticing textures,

Chapter Two: Health and Balance for Optimal Effectiveness

I had achieved more than I had expected. My reality had expanded. I had experienced a joy-filled time.

In this very simple exploration of noticing textures, I discovered that I had achieved the desired outcome of taking my observation of texture out of my non-ordinary reality and into my ordinary reality. I also achieved additional outcomes that were a surprise, giving me more than I had set out to do. I felt expanded, I had a joy-filled time, and I felt as though I was in a new and expanded reality in which I was noticing much more of what was present instead of limiting myself through my ordinary perceptual filters.

I am writing this some days later, and the feeling of expansion continues. I was looking at some cards this morning that were very familiar to me, and for the first time, the simple pictures became three-dimensional and I noticed artistic aspects in the cards that I had never seen before. I laughed, because I had the feeling of being given something new. I walked in the woods today and I had a greater noticing of everything, from rustling dry leaves to the falling of a pine cone, as though in slow motion. I am very curious about the factors that have brought about this expanded awareness. So far, I have figured out that noticing through a perceptual filter that is non-ordinary reality for me is one part of it. Ceasing the struggle of which perceptual filter is dominant is another. Having a playful approach with a heart filled with joy at the discoveries is another.

I'll backtrack just a little now to share with you my discoveries in reading the labels. I have already shared the labels "Self Esteem USA," "Divine USA," and "Mudd Jeans." I had additional fits of giggles at some of the other labels: "Limited America," which was made in Korea; "Personal," which was made in Sri Lanka; "Apostrophe," made in Indonesia; "The Limited Star Quality," made in Korea; "Planet Sleep," made in China. I realized I could weave an interesting story from the labels in relation to their place of manufacture. Such a story would include how small a global village we really are. I especially liked the self-esteem of the USA being manufactured in India.

At the cash register, I noticed a large fish tank with a pair of Oscar fish named Oscar and Myer. It was not their color that captured me, but their texture. The rust colors, the browns, creams, and blacks were beautiful, and their friendliness was evident. The texture of these fish was like velvet, a rich beautiful velvet, soft to the touch and beautiful to see. This took my breath away, and then I giggled in my joy at noticing the textures. I also realized that my biggest joy was not in the textures of the clothes, but in the texture of living beings, of nature, of something that, according to the rules I live by, is genuine.

A sign overhead caught my attention: "Life is not measured by the breaths we take, but by the moments that take our breath away." I had several moments during this hour in the thrift shop that took my breath away in sheer childlike joy from the discoveries. My conscious awareness was expanded to greater genuine contact with myself.

Note to self: practice getting into non-ordinary perceptual filters as often as possible so that it gets easier and easier to notice *reality* from different perspectives, allowing myself to expand in the process. I am guessing that with practice, sustaining the non-ordinary perceptual lenses becomes easier. If I find myself unable to shift to non-ordinary perceptual filters, remind myself to play as I did with the thrift store excursion.

Your turn.

1. If what is conveyed here is true, what would I see?
2. If what is conveyed here is true, what would I hear?
3. If what is conveyed here is true, what would I feel?
4. If what is conveyed here is true, what would I know?
5. If what is conveyed here is true, how could this affect your leadership?

Notes

A Way of Increasing Your Genuine Contact with Yourself

As you read this segment, to add experiences of your own, I invite you to reflect on

1. What color comes to mind?
2. What texture comes to mind?
3. What metaphor comes to mind?
4. What dance movement comes to mind?
5. What are you learning about genuine contact?

I think that we have made genuine contact with ourselves when we stop judging ourselves. I think that when we judge ourselves, our angels look at us and sigh, wishing we could see ourselves the way that they see us in all of our beauty. I also think that when we judge ourselves, our own spirit weeps at our self-cruelty. Somewhere along the line, I have picked up that joy is our birthright. If this is true, then when I am in genuine contact with myself, I access this joy. When I am in joy, it is not possible for me to judge myself. If you expand your awareness so that your perceptual filters expand, and you work with more and more of the multidimensional being that you are in your noticing exercises, you will discover yourself to be in genuine contact with yourself in joy.

Once you have found genuine contact with yourself, probing further will continue to reveal to you more of who you really are. There is a lot written about the shadow side of self, the unclaimed parts of the self. Often this implies qualities considered to be negative or dark that people want to keep hidden. In my experience, that is far less of a problem than people wanting to hide their strength, their power, their beautiful inner light. I think of the Marianne Williamson poem, "Our Greatest Fear."[8] In hearing this poem, we are challenged with having the strength to find our light and not to be afraid of it, saying that it is our light and not our darkness that we fear. I know you have a lot of strength that maybe you just have not yet stepped into. In this journey of genuine contact, it is time for you to access that strength.

Mental Consciousness

Developing your mental consciousness means taking command of your thoughts. Thoughts form into patterns of thought, called beliefs. Beliefs create your reality. What we focus on with our minds is what we are attracted to, and helps determine what is attracted to us. Have you ever feared something, and then had the exact thing happen? My husband, Ward, relates a story from his early twenties. He was out with a number of friends, driving their cars on the ice in a large, empty parking lot, practicing skidding in circles. His friend, Melvin, expressed fear of hitting the only obstacle in the parking lot, a tall light standard. Sure enough, he did, and in doing so, damaged his car significantly. None of the others had problems, just fun. Successful car racing drivers avoid focusing on the possibility of hitting walls, thus reducing the likelihood that they will do so.

Thoughts are expressed in words, and in getting command of your thoughts it is interesting to pay attention to your choice of words and whether the words you use actually mean what you say. For example, people often say "I am sick" or "I am tired" when what they really mean is "I feel sick" or "I feel tired." By constantly using the term "I am" in these cases, you can actually subconsciously cause yourself harm. With the "I am," you are defining yourself in ways that the subconscious then responds to. If you say, "I am sick," don't be surprised if you then are sick.

When you say "I wish," it implies that you don't believe you will get it, and you end up remaining in the state of wishing as you have defined. If you use "I intend" instead, it shows that you believe you will get it, and then you stay in a state of expectancy to support the words that you have commanded. When you say that you "should" do something, it indicates that you are doing something based on another person's value system, which is giving away your power. (For example, "I really should clean up the dishes before my mother-in-law comes over.") No matter how much you do in the realm of shoulds to please others, you will never do enough, because no matter how much you try to please others, the list of those who are not pleased is long.

Every thought is a vibration, and the vibration attracts like energy unto itself. What are you attracting with your thought vibrations? Do you like what you are attracting? You can get command over your thoughts, and whenever a thought flits through your mind that you know will serve no good purpose, simply thank that thought and ask it to move on, because you do not want that particular vibratory field of attraction. Do not push against a thought, because the more you push against it, the stronger it becomes. Truly, just thank the thought and command it to move on. These types of thoughts that are not useful are sorrow, futility, fear of defeat, fear of ruin, self-criticism, doubts, disappointments, indulgences, overextension and accompanying resentment, anxiety, oppression, worry, and fear of failure. I think you can imagine that when you expend mental energy on these kinds of thoughts, you waste energy that is then no longer available for creating the thought vibrations that you do want to attract. Command your thoughts to be solution focused, not problem focused. Solutions have very different vibrations than problems, and will attract what you do want rather than attracting what you do not want. You have the power to focus your thoughts, always, no matter what is going on around you and who is doing what. Your pattern of thought does not have to follow what is going on around you.

Getting command over your thoughts and meaning the actual words that you think and say will assist you in optimizing your mental consciousness. Another way to optimize mental consciousness is to keep your thoughts in the present, rather than holding on to resentments of the past or worries about the future. If you spend your mental energy in the past or future, there is very little left for optimal mental consciousness in the present.

Note to self: when doing my daily workout on the Wii Fit, keep my thoughts totally focused on what I am doing instead of letting them wander; discipline my thoughts to do what I want them to do.

Spiritual Consciousness

To optimize your spiritual consciousness and to benefit from the wisdom and perception of this consciousness, you will need to optimize your spiritual health. A step to doing this is practicing with your intuitive intelligence to strengthen it. There are books on intuition in our bibliography, and yet a book is not necessary, because many opportunities exist in your everyday environment to use and improve your intuition. For instance, when I guide my children through a decision, I ask them to write down all possible solutions on index cards and then to shuffle the cards and turn them upside down so that they cannot see what is written on them. They then choose a card (or more if their intuition guides them to more) that is chosen to be the solution. This is one use of intuition for making decisions. It has wonderful results, while simultaneously strengthening intuition and spiritual consciousness.

Strengthening your faith that the universe is good and that life is worth living also optimizes your spiritual consciousness. Strengthening your faith is different from giving your power away to a religion. There is a difference between spirituality and religion, and it is important to know the difference. I think that religions can assist you to strengthen your faith, and if they do so, they are worth your attention. If the religion demands that you worship it, instead of worshipping a Higher Power, there is no opportunity to strengthen your faith because you are giving your power over to that religion.

Note to self: remember to do something that you have never done as often as possible to stay open to fun and surprise as a way to strengthen my spiritual consciousness.

Emotional Consciousness

To optimize your emotional consciousness and to benefit from the wisdom and perception of this consciousness, you will need to develop awareness of your emotional state at all times. Your emotions are a guidance system for you. If you feel disharmonious emotions, the wisdom that they give you is that you are off course in relation to who you truly are. If you feel harmonious emotions, you will know you are on course with who you really are. Your feelings do not lie to you. You have a right to those feelings, and the more you can access the wisdom that those feelings are providing, the more you can guide yourself and your decisions.

The best source that I am aware of for learning to tune in to your emotional state is the advice given in the book *Ask and It Is Given*, by Esther and Jerry Hicks, based on the teachings of Abraham, a nonphysical being similar to a guardian angel. They list twenty-two emotional states.[9] In the book, they give tips on how to identify which emotional state you are in so that you can start developing your conscious awareness. They conclude the book with a series of different and very practical exercises to choose from in which you identify your emotional starting point and then do the exercise with the anticipated result of going up at least one level in the hierarchical list of emotions. For example, in their list, hatred is a step up emotionally from jealousy. They teach that it is challenging to go from one of the lower vibration emotions at the bottom of the list to one of the higher vibrations at the top of the list in one step. They encourage the reader that by achieving even one step, it is advancement of the vibratory field of the emotions.

Following their teaching assisted me greatly in achieving my current level of emotional consciousness.

Note to self: when I compromise part of myself, I abandon part of my whole self. This doesn't feel good. By paying attention to my feelings, I will monitor myself to ensure that I do not unconsciously abandon myself as per old patterns that no longer serve me (if they ever did).

Physical Consciousness

To optimize your physical consciousness and to benefit from the wisdom and perception of this consciousness, you will need to optimize your physical health. I have some ideas for you to do that I cover in the chapter on the blueprint for optimal health being in every organism. My favorite teacher about physical health is Andreas Moritz, an internationally acclaimed medical intuitive who lives in North Carolina.

Note to self: it is time to do another series of the detox cleanses that Andreas recommends in his book *Timeless Secrets of Health and Rejuvenation*.

Your turn.

1. If what is conveyed here is true, what would I see?
2. If what is conveyed here is true, what would I hear?
3. If what is conveyed here is true, what would I feel?
4. If what is conveyed here is true, what would I know?
5. If what is conveyed here is true, how could this affect your leadership?

Notes

Genuine Contact with Another

As you read this section, to add experiences of your own, I invite you to reflect on

1. What color comes to mind?
2. What texture comes to mind?
3. What metaphor comes to mind?
4. What dance movement comes to mind?
5. What are you learning about genuine contact?

Were you able to make genuine contact with another human being when you were little? Possibly your mother, your father, or a sibling was the first person that you were in genuine contact with. I think that is the ideal situation to learn the state of joy that is achieved in knowing someone and having them truly know you. The reason I think it is ideal is that if you achieved genuine contact with another human being so early in life, you have had the best possible foundation for going through life being able to be in genuine contact with other individuals that you feel a sense of harmony with. Being in genuine contact with another human being might then come more naturally to you, without being in a state of flight, fight, or paralysis when someone seeks to be close to you.

I do not think that learning to be in genuine contact with someone always comes with the initial family unit, for a number of reasons.

Chapter Two: Health and Balance for Optimal Effectiveness

It may not feel safe to be in genuine contact with immediate family members or they may not be available for genuine contact. My parents, in their late teens, were in the Second World War on the German side. They went through a lot of traumas, and so by the time they married and had me in their mid-thirties, they were not able to be in genuine contact with either each other or with me. At the time, it was also the common practice of mothers to lay an infant on a pillow instead of holding them directly skin to skin, so as better to support the back of the infant, a practice that my mother, with good intentions for me, followed. Unfortunately, this also got in the way of making genuine contact. In those days, fathers had little to do with infants, which is a practice that thankfully has changed. My father really had to stretch to be present to his grandchildren when they were infants, even willingly babysitting. He admitted to me that when I was an infant, he had not so much as pushed the buggy, because in those days men didn't participate with the rearing of the infant.

For me, there was no experience of early genuine contact with another individual. I had no siblings. As a small family unit of three, we emigrated from Germany to Canada when I was two, and the years that followed as an immigrant family struggling to make it, with real prejudice against us for being German in a geographic area that was Anglo-Saxon, limited my opportunities for genuine contact. I know that I longed for genuine contact with another human being during my early life. When I was nine years of age, I was even able to put words to this. I believe that I carried prebirth memories with me of genuine contact with Source—the experience of a profound oneness—and that the feelings of separation from this oneness were a driving force in me to find genuine contact. Remember, you don't need to believe that we all have a prebirth connection, or that we have multiple lifetimes with periods of oneness in between these lifetimes. I write from this perspective because it is mine, and you need only take from my perspective what is useful to you.

I would like to clarify that being in genuine contact and wonderfully close to someone can take place with parents, siblings, close friends, and with mates in couple relationships. We each experience a journey to be in genuine contact with another human being so that we can truly be our genuine self and be received as such unconditionally, and receive the other person for who she is, unconditionally. Even if success in this quest for one-to-one genuine contact is not achieved early in life, it can be achieved later. If you are like me, without the conditions for being in genuine contact with another early, you may have focused on being in genuine contact with Creator, with Creation, with yourself, and/or with a collective. There is no one correct order in this relationship work of genuine contact. I was able to be in genuine contact with one other as the last phase of learning to be in genuine contact.

I had moments of genuine contact with one other along the way. One source of learning to be in genuine contact with one another, early in life, is through a friend. Even better when it is possible to have several friends, each one providing the opportunity, even if they don't know it, to have the experience of being in genuine contact with another. From my early years to the present, friends taught me a lot about genuine contact with one other. Once the Genuine Contact program was launched and taught in the world, I developed incredible friendships in true genuine contact with different people who were committed to the vital importance of genuine contact. Over the years, I have had friends for shorter periods of time with whom I have made genuine contact, and then the friendship ended. I have made other friends with whom I have genuine contact on an ongoing basis, likely a lifelong basis. I anticipate that as I continue on in life, I will find more individuals to be in genuine contact with. I am learning a lot about having a limitless supply of love for my fellow humans.

Chapter Two: Health and Balance for Optimal Effectiveness

Friends are very important to me in being in genuine contact and learning lessons about what it takes to be in genuine contact with another. Sometimes friends and I are in joy together, and sometimes we feel as if we are sitting in a hot fire together. I find that attaining a state of genuine contact with a friend is not a static state of "having arrived." Rather, I have experienced genuine contact being reached, followed by the expansion and growth of one individual or both, during which I experienced gaps in genuine contact, particularly when our stages of growth differed.

In high school, a childhood friend (Deb) and I walked to the same school, and yet kept to opposite sides of the road so that we were clear with each other that we were not walking together. She was a cheerleader. I played on the school basketball and volleyball teams. She was a member of one sorority and I was a member of a rival sorority. She was cute and little and blonde. I was tall and gangly and attractive, but not cute. During that period, we were not in genuine contact with each other. As we matured, we found our way to each other again, and in university resumed our genuine contact, to last until the present, with all growth along the way being in good harmony. Was there a catalyst to bring us back into genuine contact? Without planning it, we both ended up at the same university, knew almost no one else, and turned to each other and found ourselves easily back in genuine contact.

I remember my friend, Michelle, telling me that she saw me going through a door to another level of my growth, and wanted me to know that she had chosen not to go there with me. She said she was scared of what it might involve and what this spurt in growth might mean in her life. She, as a good friend, encouraged me to go and grow. We lost genuine contact with each other for a while and then found it again. At different times in our friendship, we have repeated this pattern. It has caused tensions at times, and then we find our genuine contact with each other again. I think that we are tied with a bond of love that has seen us through our staggered growth periods.

One of my leaps in personal growth occurred when I was thirty-six. At that time, I was married and the mother of four children, ranging in age from six to twelve. For various reasons, the marriage was ending, and so we became a different family unit that involved the children being with me most of the time, and having regular visits with their father. It was a big adjustment for all of us. Somehow, the children's father and I managed to remain friends with one another despite the differences. We maintained as much genuine contact with each other as we were able to achieve. However, almost all of our friends, whom I had been in genuine contact with, dropped both of us as friends almost immediately.

One of them wrote to me two years later, saying that she apologized and wanted me to understand her point of view. She said that when I left my marriage, taking four children with me, she and most of the others were angry at me. She said that many of their own marriages were not working and that in each case they had created reasons to stay, including "for the children's sake." She and most of the others had one or two children. She said that when I left, it challenged all their excuses about why they were choosing to stay in marriages that didn't work, because I had the courage to find a way to start again, even with four children.

At another time, I lost almost all of my friends, people whom I had attracted to my life after my divorce, when I remarried. I had been in genuine contact with them. After my marriage, I was told that I had changed, and one by one the friendships ended. I was deeply saddened and also puzzled. All of these friends, during our several-year period of genuine contact, had made a point of encouraging me to grow and expand, as I had with them. We all individually and collectively actively sought change in our lives. I was puzzled that they now turned away from me because I had changed. In thinking about the

Chapter Two: Health and Balance for Optimal Effectiveness

metaphor of the crabs in the basket, I have wondered if this story in some ways applies to my situation of changing and my friends wanting to pull me back "into the basket" so that we could all stay together in the same way we had been. I think that the good feeling of being in genuine contact with each other was a feeling that they wanted to hold on to, and change implied that this feeling might be lost. I realize that we had genuine contact for a period only, so long as we all participated by a basic and implicit set of rules.

I believe that when individuals who are in genuine contact with each other are consciously committed to their growth and are in a state of grace in allowing the other to grow, genuine contact can be maintained during growth. If it is lost, it is possible to regain genuine contact at some later point. Perhaps genuine contact simply takes a back seat for a while during some growth periods. Sometimes genuine contact is reached and then lost and not attained again. Sometimes, without anyone being at fault, the mind enters into coping mechanisms that have nothing to do with the two people involved in a friendship.

Psychologists have different words for different coping mechanisms, but ones that affect genuine contact in a destructive way include when people are mentally fractured, usually through previous trauma situations, and they cannot bring their whole self to any relationship. This does not mean that all people with early traumas are fractured. They may have healed from these traumas if their minds had different ways of coping or had regained health with projection or transference. People who need to rely on their mind's coping skills, for whatever reason, struggle with genuine contact and, as I have experienced, can feel threatened by one-to-one genuine contact.

Sometimes the timing and the circumstances simply are not right. A participant in one of our workshops came up to me at the very end and grasped my hands, looking deeply into my eyes. She struggled with

English and yet wanted to convey something important to her heart. She said that at the start of our time together, she did not think she could learn from me because I reminded her of her mother (transference), and she was so happy that she had been able to learn and that my presence helped her have more peace with her mother. I was deeply moved by her healing and by the genuine contact that she and I had in that moment of sharing, genuine contact that has lasted to this day.

One of the archetypes that is strong in me is the archetype of the mother, possibly because I am a mother and a grandmother, possibly because it is in my nature, having been mastered in previous lifetimes. It is not uncommon for people to transfer onto me aspects that are not mine, but are aspects of their own mother. During this phase of transference, genuine contact doesn't happen between me and the person, because that person cannot see me for who I am. However, as with this participant, wonderful healing and genuine contact can occur as the transference dissipates as no longer necessary.

In one of our workshops, a participant stuck her legs out into the circle, almost tripping me as I was walking inside the circle of people as I was talking. I barely avoided the intentional obstacle. She folded her arms angrily and was the first to speak, declaring to all of us that we would not want her to be in genuine contact with any of us as a whole person, because we would have to deal with subjects and emotions and behaviors that were not nice. I felt the genuine contact in her approach and knew I liked her a lot. She was showing up with her genuine being. Yet, it is true; being in genuine contact does not mean always being nice. Each of us has many aspects. Being in genuine contact with one another requires being in genuine contact with the whole person.

In my first marriage, I was in genuine contact to the extent that I was able to be in genuine contact with another person at the time. I was nineteen and Doug was twenty-one. I had a lot of what I will simply refer

Chapter Two: Health and Balance for Optimal Effectiveness

to as rocks in my backpack from my past that took a lot of my attention, and so there was not a lot of me available to be in genuine contact. The same was true for Doug. Each of us was fractured from previous traumas in our lives. At the time and in our youth, we would have declared that we were in genuine contact. In hindsight, I know we were in genuine contact only to the extent that we could be at that point in our lives.

I have always been deeply grateful to Doug. To the extent that he could be in genuine contact with himself and with me, he was. Despite his childhood traumas, he was solid as a rock and unwavering, and I was able to cling to him while I set about the business of growing, expanding, and figuring out who I was. I credit Doug with giving me enough stability that I chose life at a time when I was very uncertain about life. At the time that I made a big leap in my growth, Doug had some additional traumas in his life from his birth family, and he was still dealing with these issues. I yearned for genuine contact, and at the time he could not be in genuine contact with anyone, including me and the children, due to a lot of personal pain. He has moved on since then, emerged from that state, remarried a wonderful woman, and continues his growth and expansion.

I had wonderful lessons about being in genuine contact from my children. I learned from them as newborns, as babies, as toddlers, as children, as teenagers, and now as adults. I am myself with them. And they are themselves. It is not really more complicated than that to be in this state of genuine contact. I have found that genuine contact with one another is true and unconditional love. My children opened me to this true and unconditional love, I learned about genuine contact from them, I healed into my wholeness through this unconditional love, and I now have more capacity for genuine contact with others.

The friendships that I retained deepened in their capacity for genuine contact. New friendships that I have made in more recent years have begun and have been sustained in beautiful genuine contact. I have experienced unconditional love in my friendships, learning more about a fuller capacity of genuine contact in the process.

All the people I am currently in genuine contact with feel as if they're members of my soul group. I am not an expert on soul groups; I simply believe that they exist. I recognize people and feel that I have known them for always. I simply acknowledge to myself that we must be members of the same soul group, and so we are in fact really recognizing each other at an energy level. We are mates, in the same soul group, sometimes referred to as soul mates. I don't know how many individuals make up a soul group. I believe that prebirth, we have made some kind of contract with each other, not only to find each other, but also to assist each other to fulfill our purpose on this planet. It has been easy to find members of my soul group once I started paying attention. It has been easy to get into genuine contact with members of my soul group. Within members of a soul group, the fullness of unconditional love is an incredible gift.

I have mentioned my belief in soul groups. Everyone in a soul group is a soul mate to one another in the group, and the connection between each is strong. The soul mate connection is recognizable by the feeling of knowing someone when there is usually little known history together, if any. Within the larger soul groups, there are soul twins. I am fortunate to be married to my soul twin. I recognized Ward immediately upon meeting him and knew we would become life mates. There was genuine contact from the start. As we got to know each other better in our ten-month courtship, we discovered our deep love for each other and our sense of oneness; we discovered that we often were having thoughts about the same things at the same time. We would not have identical thoughts, because we are unique. However, what could feel like a mind meld was uncanny. We have an identical sense of purpose in the world and yet different ideas about how to fulfill our purpose. We were able to bring our ideas together in a common vision for what we want to work toward. While we both have a lot of strengths, we each have aspects of ourselves that need healing. Ward has strengths where I need healing and he can use his strengths to assist me in finding my optimal health in all ways. I have strengths where he needs healing and I can use my strengths to assist Ward in finding his optimal health in all ways. We love each other and are in love with each other. I am myself with Ward, and he is fully himself with me. The genuine contact between us is growing, expanding, and nurturing for us both. We also are engaged in learning from our genuine contact with each other.

Note to self: I intend to play more with people I am in genuine contact with.

Your turn.

1. If what is conveyed here is true, what would I see?
2. If what is conveyed here is true, what would I hear?
3. If what is conveyed here is true, what would I feel?
4. If what is conveyed here is true, what would I know?
5. If what is conveyed here is true, how could this affect your leadership?

Notes

Judgment and Discernment

As you read this segment, to add experiences of your own, I invite you to reflect on

1. What color comes to mind?
2. What texture comes to mind?
3. What metaphor comes to mind?
4. What dance movement comes to mind?
5. What are you learning about genuine contact?

Prejudgment (prejudice) and judgment get in the way of genuine contact just as fear gets in the way. I experience judgment as resulting from my mental consciousness, from my thoughts. I am committed to being in genuine contact with people, and so over the years, I have chosen to understand a lot about judgment so that this would not be an unnecessary barrier in my life. Through self-discipline, I have learned that I can control my thinking by taking command over what my thoughts focus on. As I learn more and more control over what my thoughts focus on, I have fewer and fewer periods of judgment of others as either good or bad. I still fall into periods of judgment before I become aware that my thoughts have gotten scattered and that my energy is being wasted in such thoughts. I think that at best, the time I spend in judgment is now very small and I can rebalance my thoughts to be more positive quickly. In talking with friends, I've found that almost all have such periods, the need to refocus thoughts on more

Chapter Two: Health and Balance for Optimal Effectiveness

positive things and ideas, and the shortening of the time it takes to shift from discovering that the mind has wandered into judgment to achieving a different focus.

Prejudgments are those judgments that I make even before I have met a person. I might prejudge that person as good because of all that I have heard about her, or I might prejudge her as troublesome because of all that I have conjured up in my mind about her. In either case, this reduces the likelihood of genuine contact, because I am approaching the person with a barrier created by my prejudgments.

Judgments are my analysis of a person based on what my mind has done to categorize data about the person into good or bad. Judgments of good and bad also inhibit genuine contact. Once I have judged, I have made a measurement, I have categorized, I have developed assumptions to go along with the judgment, and all of this gets in the way of genuine contact.

When I focus my thoughts on achieving genuine contact, I am not in a state of prejudgment or judgment. I am simply intending to have genuine contact and then allowing it to happen. Sometimes I have genuine contact with the individual and sometimes I do not. I may have intended genuine contact without judgment, and the other person might perceive me through prejudgments and judgments. When this happens, I sometimes experience neutrality and simply move on. At other times, I feel hurt, and sometimes deeply hurt, because the person has not looked at me for who I am and has placed me in a category that doesn't feel good.

I have learned in such situations that there is nothing I can do to alter the judgments of the person about me except to keep on being me and wait for a possible shift. Any and all actions that I take to attempt to achieve genuine contact with a person who is in judgment of me have proven futile. I continue offering the person the gift of me being me, nothing more and nothing less. It is what I have to offer. I am not in this world to make anyone happy, and indeed, "making" someone happy is an impossible task. I am here to be me and to be open for genuine contact.

This does not mean that I have a large group of people that I am in genuine contact with on a regular basis, and so I want to also address the topic of discernment. I have a responsibility to manage my personal energy, to take care of my life force so that it does not get depleted, and to have energy available for fulfilling my purpose on this planet. Even when I achieve genuine contact and there are no barriers to the genuine contact, not every person that I have ever been in genuine contact with is someone that I spend time with on a regular basis. I include all people with whom I have ever been in genuine contact in my prayers every morning, because each has been valuable to me and to my growth and expansion. I manage who I am in regular contact with through discernment about my energy.

To assist people in understanding about discernment, Ward uses ice cream as a metaphor. He says that discernment is about knowing that there are differences in the flavors. For example, one is chocolate, one is strawberry, one is vanilla. Discernment includes having a personal preference for strawberry. Judgment would come if a person says vanilla is good but chocolate and strawberry are bad. I hope you can understand the difference. Judgment gets in the way of genuine contact. Discernment allows for genuine contact and allows me to make choices of who I feel in the most harmony with and thus want to spend time with. Discernment does not mean that others with whom I have engaged are good or bad. It simply means that I am managing my own energy and I choose those I wish to engage with and those I don't, simply by how energized I feel in being with one person and how depleted I feel in being with another person. In both cases, I may be in genuine contact with the person.

The great Sufi poet Rumi wrote about judgment by saying: "Out beyond ideas of rightdoing and wrongdoing, there is a field. I will meet

Chapter Two: Health and Balance for Optimal Effectiveness

you there." Until I was in my thirties, I ran into significant challenges in my one-to-one relationships, because I was out in that field and did not have the comprehension that others were not out in that field beyond wrongdoing and rightdoing. I discovered that I would get hurt by something that came at me as someone was judging me, and I didn't see this judgment coming. At one point, I went for counseling help and the therapist said that I would not graduate from therapy until I had learned to be cynical. I just couldn't get it. He wanted me to learn to be in judgment of others so that I could protect myself better. Today, I watch my young grandchildren and witness their total lack of judgment and wonder how and when they will start judging others, if at all.

At about forty, having become totally confused between being too open and being in judgment, I discovered that in the heat of emotionally charged moments, my thoughts categorized the other person as bad or good. I was, indeed, in judgment. This assisted with some self-protection of my heart by not getting too close to anyone who was "bad." It did not assist with what my heart and soul knew to be true, which was that inside every person, there was an inner core of good. My internal battle to figure out how to be less vulnerable to pain and yet how to be open and in genuine contact was frustrating and took up a lot of my energy at different times.

At forty-four, I met Ward, and he has been my greatest teacher about boundaries, managing my energy, and using discernment regarding who I want to engage with and for how long. I found his approach suited me and ended my frustration. I can look at the beautiful light in each person, and without judgment, I can discern that my energy field and that of another person are not harmonious, so being in relationship with them is an energy drain. It does not make either one of us good or bad in the situation. I am simply able to discern what is right for my energy, and thus I can adhere to my energy management boundaries.

On occasion, the person who is an energy drain for me is a family member or a close friend who sits in judgment of me. I take a deep breath and sigh, because this is an extremely challenging situation. I do not want to disengage from the person, although there is no genuine contact possible when judgment is present. Sometimes I feel deep love for the person. Sometimes I feel hurt by the judgment. Usually, I shift into paralysis or desire for flight because I do not know what to do. When any of us have a desire for flight because of fear, and we do not act on our desire for flight because our mind overrides this desire with words like "but she is my mother," then the body gets quite confused. It has the physiological response to flee and it is being held in the situation by the will of the mind. If this lasts long enough, the body ends up with illness, a situation I would rather not experience.

I wish that I could tell you that I have figured out how to handle this sort of situation. I have not. Sage advice would be for me to be willing to disengage from relationships with non-harmonious family members and close friends when genuine contact is not possible. This has not felt easy for me to do, and so I am still working on guidance for myself regarding this type of situation. So far, I have gotten as far as letting those close to me know what my personal rules of engagement are for me to be able to fully engage. This has alleviated some situations. In others, this only added to the judgment that I was facing.

I wish that I could pose the following questions to the person who is judging me harshly. Because I don't feel that I can do so, I pose them to myself, and sometimes this also alleviates the situation so that I know what I need to do to manage my energy.

- Do you love yourself?
- Do you know yourself?

- Do you know how powerful you are? Do you know that your power ends where your fear begins?
- Can you stop blaming yourself? Me? God?
- Do you feel trapped?
- Can you believe that the universe is a benevolent place that will provide you with what you need and want?
- Can you be in conversations in your search for your answers, accepting that everything you hear comes from a perceptual bias and from a particular rule set and is actually a story, not a truth or a lie? Are you consciously aware of your rule set? We all have them.

Note to self: stay open to answers about what to do when a family member or close friend is sitting in judgment of me and I cannot feel any genuine contact. I recognize that in these situations, I fear loss, and sometimes my fear of loss is not about this person but about others who are connected with us. I fear losing others whom I love deeply and am in genuine contact with. I still struggle with understanding that I am loved unconditionally by these others or else I would not fear. In my fear, I have allowed myself to have a pattern of feeling trapped because I do not honor my flight response. I have had physical symptoms resulting from this spiritual and emotional entrapment by myself.

As I sit here and write, I realize that the answer lies in my judgment of myself. When I am in judgment of myself, am I in genuine contact with myself? Probably not. I will go back to my writing about genuine contact with myself and explore whether I am walking my talk. It seems to me that if I am not judging myself, I would disengage from a family member or friend that I am not in harmony with because of feeling judged, and that I would love myself unconditionally, knowing that if there are any losses of people in my life as a result of my choices, it is okay.

Your turn.

1. If what is conveyed here is true, what would I see?
2. If what is conveyed here is true, what would I hear?
3. If what is conveyed here is true, what would I feel?
4. If what is conveyed here is true, what would I know?
5. If what is conveyed here is true, how could this affect your leadership?

Notes

Genuine Contact with a Collective

As you read this segment, to add experiences of your own, I invite you to reflect on

1. What color comes to mind?
2. What texture comes to mind?
3. What metaphor comes to mind?
4. What dance movement comes to mind?
5. What are you learning about genuine contact?

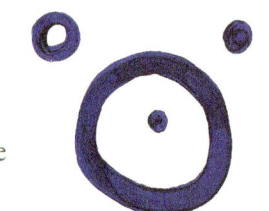

Finding Your Way to Achieving Genuine Contact with a Collective

Another arena for your development and expansion is the arena of the collective, allowing yourself to make genuine contact with a collective of people. The collective that you know best is likely your family. You may or may not have figured out how to be in genuine contact with your family. They might know you well, and vice versa. Another possibility is that they do not know you and they only know the family story that they have created about who they think you are. Your family may or may not be a collective that you choose to be in genuine contact with. It is not a requirement. However, being in genuine contact with some type of collective enhances your growth.

Chapter Two: Health and Balance for Optimal Effectiveness

In my development, I was not able to make genuine contact with a collective through my family of origin. I am an only child, and my parents stopped being a unit when I was very young. With the three of us being immigrants in Canada with no other family members in the country, there was simply no family collective to relate to. I longed for one, and I longed for the genuine contact within such a collective.

Sometimes my efforts to make genuine contact with a collective have been joyful, at least for a time. I say at least for a time because almost every collective I have participated in has at some point been fraught with divisiveness, and then my joy has gone out of my participation. In some situations, I discovered that the collective then went on just fine without me and that the divisiveness was within me, because I was not in alignment with the values of the collective. I think of a women's group that I was part of that was vested in raising the profile of women leaders. I was in alignment, with joy. Then a new energy emerged in the group, with different values, that brought about a silent agreement that to be part of the group, participants also had to dislike men. Possibly you also have experienced these silent agreements that are never actually spoken, and yet you know that if you do not stay within the silent agreement, what I refer to as the political correctness of the group, you will be shunned and treated as an outsider.

I think we are at a time in our human story when we are figuring out how to operate within collectives within which we can make genuine contact by bringing our whole self into the collective, being accepted for the wholeness of who we are, and accepting others in ways that are life-nurturing and non-judgmental. I am not talking about the collectives within which you can only retain your place if you hide some of who you are so that you fit within the political correctness of the collusion of the group.

A very long time ago when I was eleven years old, my father first asked me which I think is stronger—love or hate. I have always answered that love is stronger. At this time, my father is eighty-eight years old and continues to ask me if I have figured out the answer to this question. I continue to answer that love is stronger. He continues to shake his head and say that history does not support my belief. His view is that sometimes humans have a truce between wars, battles, and conflicts of all sorts, and that it is not actually peace. He says that from the beginning, man has been against man and that some form of conflict has been continuous. The intervals of truce are filled with fear, and man is not absent from fear during these periods. If man did not have fear during truce or peaceful times, then nations would fearlessly disarm, neighbors would fearlessly unlock their doors, and cities would not need their police. He asks me if what I see supports love as being stronger. I say that man is evolving and this is a new age, and maybe in this new age we will figure out how love can prevail. He asks me if I think I will see it in my lifetime. I have to admit to him that I do not know, but that when I look into the eyes of my granddaughters, I believe that if we do things differently now, they might see love as the stronger force in their lifetimes.

Genuine Contact with Family

Perhaps it was my father's questioning at the age of eleven that set me on the path of finding an answer to love being the stronger force. Somewhere deep inside me, despite his skepticism, I knew my

Chapter Two: Health and Balance for Optimal Effectiveness

answer was right despite plenty of evidence to the contrary. This was at a time in my life when I could look at every human being and see—yes, actually see—the goodness and love in them. I had many shocking experiences along the way when the behavior I experienced from some of these people did not line up with the beautiful light I saw in them. It actually took me until some time in my thirties to understand that I had not personally brought about these behaviors and that there was indeed a misalignment in the person between their beautiful inner core and their behavior. Whew. What a learning experience that was. I remember saying to people, "I wish that you could know how the angels see you," because I believed that the angels could also see the beauty in the person underneath their sometimes misguided behavior.

I made a choice. It was to either believe my father's conclusion that hate was the stronger force or to do something with my life to show that love was the stronger force. My choice was to do something that showed that love was the stronger force. I had a few setbacks, including a marriage that ended. My father asked me which force was winning inside me. I regrouped from my disappointments and said that love was the stronger force. My ex-husband and I developed a relationship of friendship, and definitely not hate. The experience left me with new knowledge about genuine contact that was unsettling. My first husband was the oldest of seven children. I thought I was part of the collective when I married him, only to discover that they did not actually know me, and that I had not brought my whole self into the marriage because I knew my whole self would be rejected by my ex-husband and by his family. I so badly wanted to be part of a family that I was willing to compromise significant parts of myself so that I could belong. In the end, when I discovered I could no longer abandon parts of myself, the marriage ended and I understood the price that I paid for my inability to bring my whole self into the marriage and into the collective with genuine contact.

By then we had had four children, and yes, it is possible to have physical contact without genuine contact, which includes your whole self in all its vulnerability. We had the amount of love in the marriage that we were each capable of at the time, both of us from home situations where we did not have the basis to experience unconditional love. I had the opportunity to form a collective of the four children and myself when they were ages seven, eight, eleven, and thirteen. They had visits with their father, of course. Yet it was the children and I that made up a collective unit after the divorce. I am forever grateful to these four children for teaching me about a collective that works, with unconditional love among each member of the collective.

They, particularly as teenagers, tested me with every possible lesson that they could provide, and just slightly short of any of them ending up in jail or in a serious car accident. We will share some of those stories in the GC Way virtual home as you get to know each of us. I know that as adults, they recently had an evening together in which they enjoyed great hilarity over things that they did that their mother didn't find out about. I think you can get the picture. They got into lots of difficult spots with some decisions they made, such as David and Aaron sneaking out a window in the middle of the night to get ice cream. They also did lots of things that were amazing and wonderful, such as always standing up for their values. They stood by each other and me, and they argued a lot too.

Sibling rivalry was sometimes more than I could deal with, and the surest way to stop the arguing among them was to use my power as a mother to let them all know there would be consequences if they kept it up. It was at that moment that the four would put their differences aside, because they immediately formed an intact unit when dealing with the authority figure of mother. And at other times, particularly when out on adventures, which we had plenty of, we experienced our joy as a collective. Through this collective, I learned about unconditional love. I had always loved my children unconditionally. I also experienced their unconditional love for me and for each other and with other humans; this was brand-new learning for me.

Some time ago, I discovered that I had a need to have a big and serious talk with my son-in-law, Phil. I am also a mother-in-law, after all. This was the kind of talk that mothers-in-law seem to need to have when they feel that something is wrong. Phil agreed to the talk, but told Rachel that our family was not normal because we liked to talk things through instead of ignoring issues. I arrived, and he met me at the door, quickly thrusting my infant granddaughter into my arms, knowing my heart would melt. I thought it was a great strategy and appreciated holding her. And then I handed her to her mom and approached Phil about our talk. He looked at me, moving his feet nervously, and said he was agreeable to the talk but didn't know how to go about having it. He said that in his family, everything was always swept under the rug, and so this business of talking something over was new to him. He did well in the talk. We agreed that we could move forward just fine and I am noticing that he seems to initiate talks now.

We recently celebrated Aaron's wedding to Steph, allowing us an occasion to bring all of the big patchwork family together. I have such joy at these occasions amid all the love and hugs. As a testament to love prevailing in this collective that makes genuine contact, Doug's wife Bonnie-Jean came and had a big talk with me. She expressed her deep appreciation for her total acceptance into our family, and how for the first time, she felt like she had a real family that genuinely accepted each other, including her. There were tears in her eyes. I looked at her and said, "Of course." She looked at me and said, "But it is not what I was expecting," and gave me a big hug. Personally, I think she makes a great wife for Doug and a terrific bonus-mom to my children, and for this I am grateful to her. She is an important member of our collective.

Rachel's Story
(written when she was twenty-one)

Following is a story that Rachel wrote when she was twenty-one, posting it to the Open Space Technology community's Listserv. The Open Space she refers to is the Open Space within which she can be genuinely herself, and associates it with the meeting method Open Space Technology that creates a container for genuine contact in a collective.

As Open Space has evolved, many people have begun to wonder if this would be a good way to raise children. Having been raised in a world of Open Space, I think that I am pretty qualified to say that the answer is an emphatic yes.

Anyone who practices Open Space knows that it very quickly becomes more than just the meeting methodology that it was originally intended to be. It quickly becomes a way of life. For many people, I think the logical question becomes, "How do I implement this in my family life?"

Even though the term Open Space hadn't been defined as Open Space when I was born, I think that all of my life has been in Open Space. For me, the definition of living in Open Space is living in an environment that has been created to allow me to access my creative self, an environment which has been safe enough for me to learn to be my authentic self. It is living in a space that has appropriate structure to grow and define my individuality.

I don't want to give the impression that Open Space is some kind of new religion or cult, but Open Space has also allowed me to access Spirit in ways that I never understood were possible. Organized religions have never been for me. That is not to say that they are wrong or that everyone should walk away from them. They just weren't right for me. When space is opened, it seems to me that it allows a space for Spirit to enter. It allows for a great and spiritual journey to begin. Open Space and Spirit are combined for me, as will be reflected in the story that follows.

I think it would be very hard to commit yourself to raising your children in Open Space. There are already so many worries as a parent, but to add Open Space to the mixture would be very scary. For those who have facilitated Open Space Technology meetings, you will understand the fear. You work so hard to create an event that lasts for only a few days. In those days you have to somehow hold the space for the people. There are many occasions where you want to interfere. To give the answers that the people are looking for instead of waiting for them to empower themselves and find their own answer. Imagine trying to hold that space for your children. To hold it for a lifetime. As a parent you have to interfere sometimes; if there is danger to your children or to others, and perhaps only if there is danger. Imagine wanting to interfere and knowing that it is your job to hold the space and let your children grow in the controlled chaos that you have created for them. For those who have the courage, I applaud you and wish you well.

To be the child living in Open Space is also scary. But I don't think it is as bad. As a participant in an Open Space Technology meeting, there is fear. For many of the participants, it is the first time in their lives that anyone has given them control. To have control over what you do and what you say. To have control over your own future. To be able to make choices to make things better instead of just grumbling with your colleagues over how you wish things could be. There is fear of having to choose what you will do and what you will say. There is fear of having control over your own future. There is fear of making choices, because your choices might not make things better. Your choices might not be the right ones. What will you do if your choices aren't the right ones?

To be the child living in Open Space isn't as scary as being a participant in an Open Space Technology meeting, in the beginning. In the innocence of childhood, you don't realize that this isn't the norm. I lived in happy bliss. I was able to make my own decisions, with the guidance of my parent, of course. I was encouraged to follow my heart. I wanted to take ballet lessons, so I took ballet lessons. I wanted to switch to tap dancing, so I switched to tap dancing. I wanted to learn to play the piano, so we bought a piano and I took lessons. I hit 13 and didn't want to be a part of that anymore, so I stopped. There was no pressure. It wasn't something I wanted to do anymore, so it was finished. And that was OK.

I was never afraid to make my own decisions. I'm sure that being that young, there was a lot of guidance from my parents, but, in the end, I was still the decision-maker. I learned a lot about making decisions and the consequences of those decisions when I was very young. We joke now about how my parents used to bribe us when we were kids, but I think it was a very effective learning tool. As a child I had a piggy bank. It wasn't like an ordinary piggy bank; in fact, I'm pretty sure it was a Mason jar. When I was good or did things that were helpful, I got to put a poker chip in the jar. When I was bad or did things that were destructive, mom got to take a poker chip out of the

Chapter Two: Health and Balance for Optimal Effectiveness

jar. When there were 100 chips in the jar, I got to go to the toy store and pick out a new toy. It was a really great learning for me. I think that those chips have had a lifelong impact on me. I certainly weigh out my decisions before making them. And to this day, I reward myself with a new toy (usually clothes or CDs) when I've been especially good.

Being in the safe environment that Open Space creates also taught me to be my authentic self. I have never been afraid to give voice to what I believe in. I have never been afraid to take responsibility for what has heart and meaning for me. I think I was about eight or nine the first time I realized that there could be upsetting consequences for me if I were to choose to live my life that way. It never occurred to me that there was any other way, and I was very shocked to learn that everyone didn't live like this. But even then, I knew that it was the way it should be.

When I was very young, we lived in a tiny community of about 1,000 people. Everyone knew everyone. There was some sort of common bond that united everyone, and often it was the children. There were about 20 or 25 kids my age in the community. We all went to the same preschool and all entered kindergarten together. At that age, you don't comprehend the cliques that develop in society, so everyone is a friend regardless of their differences. But eventually something happens that shatters the belief that everyone is equal, and you go your separate ways. For me, it was the new girl that moved into the neighborhood. She had a lot of money and a cool house. She was pretty and thin, and absolutely perfect. Everyone wanted to be her friend, including me. And we all were, except for a few.

She may have seemed absolutely perfect, but she wasn't really. She was a born leader, which isn't such a bad thing, except that it made her very bossy as a child. It was her way or no way. I couldn't understand or accept the concept of someone else telling me what to do. I didn't want to accept it, and very promptly rejected it. I don't think anyone had ever done that to her, and if they had, I'm sure the exact same thing happened to them as did to me. I rejected her control and she rejected me. In her rejection of me, everyone else rejected me. Suddenly, I was part of the few and didn't understand why. I couldn't understand why everyone would band together like that and just arbitrarily decide not to be my friend anymore. The solution was simple, right? Let her have the control and I could have all my friends back. But it wasn't that simple. I couldn't go back on my beliefs. Even at that young age I was clear that I wasn't going to give up control over my own life, even if it meant forsaking all those friends.

The events that unfolded in my teenage years were also greatly affected by Open Space. In my childhood I had the appropriate structure that was needed. It helped me to feel safe, to learn to make decisions and understand that there were consequences to my decisions. Through Open Space and the wisdom of my parents, I was encouraged to follow what had passion for me. The structure grew as I grew. Because I was small, there was very little room in the structure for chaos, but it was still there.

Then, quite suddenly, I was a teenager. And for those of you who are waiting with bated breath, no, being raised in this way does not stop "teenage rebellion" from happening. We all reach a point in our lives when we have to claim our independence. For those of you who remember those years, you'll remember that I did the teenage rebellion thing quite well.

Chapter Two: Health and Balance for Optimal Effectiveness

At that age there seemed to be two types of parents. There were those parents who were very involved with their children's lives, and in most cases, very controlling of their children's every move. Their children worked very hard, either to try to live up to their parents' every expectation or to make sure they lived up to none of it. There were also the parents who didn't seem to care about their children. Those children also worked very hard, in this case to get their parents to notice them. They either did everything to perfection or did everything "bad" that they could to draw attention to themselves.

My mom didn't fall into either category. She was very involved in our lives. But she worked very hard not to try to control us, and didn't set up unrealistic expectations of us. She also didn't try to control our friends, and didn't expect too much of them either. As a result, my mom was, and still is, known as the "cool" mom.

She allowed us the space and at the same time the security to experiment with new things. Some of these experiments were good, and she gave her approval. Some of these experiments weren't so good, and she expressed her displeasure. But she was never disapproving, and that gave us the courage to continue to explore new things. Structure grew as we grew. She held the space and made the decisions that she felt were best. She counseled us in our grief and shared in our joy. By all means, it wasn't perfect, but it was better than most situations.

While I was growing, my friends were also growing, or trying to, at least. They too were doing their best to become adults. They too were trying new things, and trying to decide what they wanted to do with their lives. However, it was a vastly different situation for them. Most of my friends had the kind of parents that didn't really care. Most of my friends were making the kinds of decisions that lead to bad behavior in order to get attention. And it worked. More often than not, the interaction they had with their parents was a lot of yelling. And even when they made good decisions, their parents never gave them any credit.

It was the first time in my life that I was in a position to observe how other people interacted with their parents. It was really very shocking to realize that everyone didn't have the same kind of relationship with their parents that I did. It was really very upsetting to realize that not everyone was encouraged to follow their hearts and to make the right decisions. I was very grateful that I had the opportunities and support that I did.

Eventually, we all got through those years. Many of the people that I was friends with are still struggling to find their independence and their identity now that they are in their twenties and living on their own. I realize that we all struggle to know who we really are for our entire lives, but for a lucky few, like me, as young adults we have a good basis of where to start. It was a great shock to me to realize that not everyone has that base.

In my last year of high school, my mom faced what I think was one of her greatest challenges in holding the space for me. I had already decided that I was going to go to college and not university. I had already decided that I wanted to get into the media, but I wasn't sure where. Radio? Newspaper? Magazine? The Internet? An ad agency? Or television? My parents had committed to paying for my college education, but there wasn't enough money for room and board. So I thought that my choices were limited to those schools that were within driving distance of home (Hamilton, Ontario). And then, my dad decided to move

Chapter Two: Health and Balance for Optimal Effectiveness

to Calgary, Alberta. It never occurred to me that I could move that far away to go to school until my mom suggested it. What a courageous and unselfish thing for her to do. And it was the decision I made. She was able to hold the space for me to decide to move to the other side of the country, leaving everything I had ever known behind, to follow my heart.

I moved in July 1997, at the age of 18. I was living with my dad, but I had to learn a whole new way of being. To an extent my mom continued, and continues, to hold the space for me. But, without really understanding it, I had to learn to hold the space for myself. To be truly independent. My journey has been incredible, like a roller coaster ride, up and down, with many, many loop-de-loops, first going slowly, then suddenly quite quickly, and then slowing down again. Through the encouragement and safety I received, I am following my heart. Every day I go to work in an incredible community, knowing that I am still learning and doing exactly what I should be doing.

The principles of Open Space have taught me so much. If a situation arises that I want to be a part of, I don't walk away from it. I find a way to make it work. I don't waste my time wondering about the "could haves" or the "what if I hads." If something isn't serving me, I'm not afraid to walk away from it, confident that there is something else that I should be doing.

And at the same time, Open Space has brought Spirit and an incredible serenity to my life. I know that whatever happens is the only thing that could have. But I also know that I was the one who allowed those things to happen. I created those situations. I am responsible for whatever happened. I am making the choices that allow me to learn the lessons that I need to learn, and to do the work that I am meant to do.

I'm not sure how much of my upbringing was a result of good parenting and how much of it was a result of living in Open Space. I'm not even sure that the two are different things. I think they complement each other quite well. I think they are really entwined in a way that is inseparable. Being the facilitator in a group is much like being a parent. You have to find your way somehow. You want to help, but not control. Open Space gives you the tools to do it.

The journey has been hard. Making the decisions that are true to you aren't always the easy ones. In fact, it has been my experience that they are often the harder choices. But they are the rewarding choices in the end. I know that I am doing what is right for me, and that is the most important thing. This is not to say that all of my choices in life have been perfect. In fact, I've made some pretty stupid choices. But I've also had the courage to recognize that those choices were wrong and to do something about them.

For as long as I can remember, I have been encouraged to follow my heart and dream. I have spent the last few years following that path, uncertain of where it may lead. The encouragement to do only what I have passion for has led me on a very scary journey, moving away from my family and all that I knew to live on the other side of the country. Spending time in other countries and unfamiliar places in order to learn and grow. Taking the plunge into a business that still has the attitude of it being "men's work" in order to make a difference. None of this could have happened if I hadn't had the support and encouragement that my family, and in turn Open Space, provides.

This support is beyond the love and support that a mother can provide. It has been in seeing what wonderful things can

Chapter Two: Health and Balance for Optimal Effectiveness

happen when you trust in the principle that whatever happens is the only thing that could happen that has given me the courage to follow my heart. Being given the space to make my own decisions about what has heart and meaning for me, and being given the support of knowing that someone thinks that I and my wisdom are precious has allowed me to access creative parts of myself, and to find what I love to do. Open Space allows the participants the chance to have a vision of their future, the future as it could be if we follow the path that we are on, and the future that could be if we follow the path we want to take. Being given this chance of seeing how the future could be is a great blessing and a hardship at the same time. The choices that are made to follow the right path are not always easy, and telling yourself that there is joy at the end of the journey does not always help.

Even though I don't live with my mother anymore, and haven't for some time now, Open Space still affects my life on a daily basis. It is not just a technique for meetings; it is a way of life, and I am living it. I know that it isn't the easiest way to live. Facing your truth and living it is hard. I've lost friends because of it. I've moved halfway across the country to follow my dream, leaving everything I knew behind because of it. It has probably been the source of a lot of my pain. But no matter how bad things seem sometimes, I've learned to trust that it is all happening because it is what needs to happen. I've learned that with the pain there is also much joy. I've learned that being your authentic self is the only way to live, even if it can be the hard way. It is the best way. Not only can you look yourself in the mirror every morning, you can enjoy what you see.

Thank you, Mom,
Love, Rachel

Note to self: I choose to continue to pay attention to ever-increasing amounts of open space for my adult children, finding ways to enjoy our wonderful love bonds and engagement with each other, while not interfering with the way they are creating their lives.

Genuine Contact with Other Collectives

After a lot of learning about what brings me joy in participating in collectives and the contrast I experience when participating in other collectives where I do not feel joy, I now choose collectives that I carefully discern, that I can align my energies with, and that I am willing to be in genuine contact with. At some time in my development in the future, I might be able to align myself with any collective. At my present level of development in making genuine contact with a collective, I do not know if this is what the future will hold for me. And so for now, I am interested in collectives that gather for harmonious, beautiful enhancement on this planet. This type of collective can be found in industry of all kinds, governments, religious groups, development agencies, civic groups, service agencies, and families. I am not interested in aligning myself or my energies with collectives that have emerged out of fear or hatred. This type of collective can also be found in any of the collectives I just mentioned. The former, when everyone shows up with the right use of their personal power and they have moved past arguing for their limitations as individuals and as a group, have unlimited potential to achieve harmonious,

Chapter Two: Health and Balance for Optimal Effectiveness

beautiful enhancement for the beings on this planet, as well as for the planet herself.

We have a lot to learn about work in collectives so that the collective continues with its momentum without getting divided. There are implications for the state of being of each member in the collective, personal motivations and agendas needing to be in alignment with the bigger purpose of the collective, a clear and true purpose that guides all actions and decisions, values-based leadership that might mean co-leadership, the creation of compelling visions that simultaneously allow individuals within the collective to achieve personal visions, the community that must allow for the whole person to show up, the management activities that must align with the purpose and vision, and agreed-upon rules of engagement for all of the relationships involved.

The State of Being of Each Member

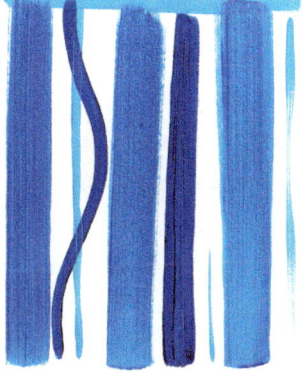

I have discovered that it is easier and more fulfilling to make genuine contact with collectives that are made up of members who are committed to their own growth, development, and learning, and who are not afraid to figure out how to be all that they can be. It is a lot easier, because in collectives like this, when someone is struggling with what might be called a shadow aspect of themselves, the members accompany the person in her growth but do not rescue her or otherwise judge the situation as anything but a stage in growth. I do not think that the people within a collective in which I feel comfortable have to have arrived at some particular state. In fact, I get a little nervous when people believe that they have arrived at some elevated state, because to me this is like an announcement that if I cannot meet their expectations, I won't fit. Because I carry out my life to the best of my ability in ways that do not attempt to meet any "shoulds" of another person that are not part of what I am guided to be or do, I am not interested.

Personal Motivations and Agendas in Alignment with the Bigger Purpose of the Collective

Everyone has their personal motivations as to why they do things and why they engage in things. You have yours and I have mine. We also each have our sense of purpose. I choose to make genuine contact with collectives to whom I feel my sense of purpose and my motivations in life are in alignment. This is one of my points of discernment for aligning with some collectives and not with others. When I make my choices, it is not about deciding that one is good and another is somehow bad. It is not my place to make a judgment like that. I can only discern in relation to my sense of alignment.

A Clear and True Purpose for the Collective

Every collective has a purpose for having attracted a grouping of people. In discerning my alignment with a collective, I want to know

Chapter Two: Health and Balance for Optimal Effectiveness

what its purpose is and whether it focuses its energy in carrying out its purpose. A minor example in my life that required discernment was joining a book club when I moved to North Carolina. I was eager to make friends in my new home and had been told a book club was a great way to do so. For a few meetings, I experienced a lot of joy. I faithfully read the book of the month, made notes, and came ready to discuss the book. Most of the women present sipped their wine during the discussions and I sipped my sparkling mineral water. I felt there was alignment, rapport. I was interested in being in genuine contact with this group of women. They made a change, announcing that they wanted to start meeting in a bar for the monthly meetings and made jokes about not needing the books anymore, as long as there was wine and good conversation. I stopped attending, as the alignment for me (purpose) was gone.

Quite often in the sector of civic organizations and nonprofit agencies, one purpose is stated for the collective in the organization to work on and a totally different purpose is financed. The organization, needing ongoing sources of funding to survive, applies for and accepts monies that are not about fulfilling its purpose. And now the collective, in order to continue working with the organization, ends up saying the organization exists for one purpose when in fact its work is on a different purpose altogether in order to continue to receive the funding. It is outside of its integrity and its internal alignment, and fractures occur as a result. I choose not to get into a collective that states one purpose and operates out of a different purpose, however well-intentioned it all may be. This is a recipe in which the collective cannot be in genuine contact with itself, because it is living a lie.

Values-Based Leadership

I am interested in being in genuine contact with collectives that have a commitment to values-based leadership. They might not have figured it all out yet. There is certainly not just one way to achieve values-based leadership. I am willing to be there for the journey. I feel alignment when the spirit of intent of the collective is for values-based leadership, particularly of a kind where leadership of service is part of the picture.

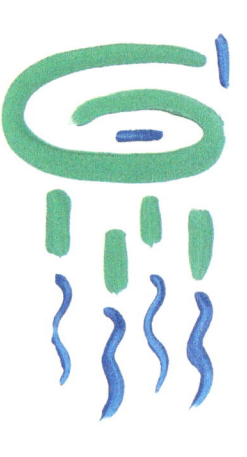

Compelling Visions that Allow Individuals to Achieve Personal Visions

Just as everyone has a sense of their purpose for existing, they also have a vision for their lives. Yes, some people argue for their limitations and make themselves smaller than they are, or even align themselves with victimhood rather than personal power. Even so, underneath all of that is a dream, a vision. A sure way to discover that dream or vision is to ask the person what he or she dreamed of being when they were young. Genuine contact is possible in collectives that have a compelling vision to which people can feel alignment with their vision for themselves.

Community Allowing the Whole Person to Be Present

Recently at a mentoring circle of Genuine Contact professionals, my friend Sabine posted the topic "being in Genuine Contact does not mean always being nice." That stirred up a lot of conversation and there were a larger number of incidents of people saying things that were unkind than might be expected. A tension was in the air. It was almost as if a sacred cow had been declared not to exist. I was fascinated, because the people gathered were very much in tune with creating the conditions for the whole person to show up and be present, and to be in genuine contact. And so what happened here? Was there some kind of unspoken illusion that genuine contact would feel good and comfortable and peaceful all the time? I think that when people feel they belong in a particular collective, it is more likely that what might be called shadow aspects will come to the surface. The reason for this is that when a person truly feels comfortable being their whole self, any unclaimed part of them will come to the surface to be faced, and to be healed into the wholeness of the person. As humans, we often need others to be mirrors for us so that we can do this examination and healing. I am in alignment with collectives that allow the whole person to be present, whatever might arise from that … allowing the collective to be real together.

In other workshops, I have experienced people expressing a lot of resistance to the idea of allowing the whole person to be present in a collective, especially if the collective is a workplace. I have often heard the cliché "leave your personal life at the door." I often wonder if a person leaving their personal life at the door also means that along with their personal life, they leave their best ideas at the door ... the very ideas that could have taken that organization to a much higher level of performance.

Management Activities Aligning with the Purpose and Vision

I also watch for whether management activities seem to be in alignment with fulfilling the purpose and achieving the vision of the collective. Maybe it is because I am getting older, but I simply do not have any desire to expend time on management work for any collective that is busywork that gets the collective no closer to its vision. I find this is another stumbling block to being able to make genuine contact with a collective. Management work that is not in alignment with getting the vision accomplished would require me to put a nice face on and roll up my sleeves to participate in tasks that have no interest to me and that would not be genuine.

Agreed-Upon Rules of Engagement for All the Relationships Involved

The last aspect of a collective that I take into account when I am discerning whether I want to be in genuine contact with it is its rules of engagement. Every collective has rules of engagement, whether it is in industry, the private sector, the public sector, the religious sector, or family. Members within the collective sometimes know what the rules of engagement or the psychological contracts are. Members sometimes, but not commonly, make conscious decisions about whether they can be their genuine selves within those rules of engagement. From my perspective, there are two levels of discernment that I go through. I do not like collectives that do not make their rules of engagement explicit. It is simply too much work for me to figure out all the implicit, silent rules of engagement. Before I know it, I have violated one or another, and I don't experience joy in those situations. The other level of discernment is whether the actual rules of engagement in a collective are ones I can be my genuine self within.

Note to self: as I learn, I want to keep redefining my rules of engagement so that I do not become rigid.

Your turn.

1. If what is conveyed here is true, what would I see?
2. If what is conveyed here is true, what would I hear?
3. If what is conveyed here is true, what would I feel?
4. If what is conveyed here is true, what would I know?
5. If what is conveyed here is true, how could this affect your leadership?

Notes

Genuine Contact with Creation, with Creator, with Source

As you read this section, to add experiences of your own, I invite you to reflect on

1. What color comes to mind?
2. What texture comes to mind?
3. What metaphor comes to mind?
4. What dance movement comes to mind?
5. What are you learning about genuine contact?

Finding Genuine Contact with Source

People find themselves in genuine contact with Source in different ways, along different paths, each individual finding the path that is exactly right for her. If someone tries to convince you to take a particular path, run fast the other way. That person, by insisting that there is only one right path, reduces the likelihood that you will find the right way for you. If you choose a particular religion or belief structure for making genuine contact with Source, do so because it feels right to you. It is not useful to your well-being to take a path to please someone else or from any notion of guilt if you want to choose differently. Guilt

Chapter Two: Health and Balance for Optimal Effectiveness

or feeling you "should" is a sure way of not being able to make genuine contact with Source. The best measure of knowing it is right for you is your feeling of joy in being on that particular path that is felt from internal and not external nudges. It is also difficult to be in genuine contact with Source if you believe that you are not good enough to have your own direct communication with Source. I assure you that you are deeply loved and that you are invited into genuine contact, into a feeling of hearts together in oneness.

You might find your connection through running, standing, walking, sitting, or lying down. It might be through meditation, yoga, tai chi, working out with your Wii Fit, singing, dancing, drawing, expressing yourself through a medium like pottery-making or painting, listening to music, listening to the rustle of leaves, or while on a busy train with hustle-and-bustle noises all around you. Each of us is different. You might feel your connection via your mental, emotional, spiritual, or physical consciousness, or through a combination of more than one aspect of your total consciousness. Whatever works for you is exactly right as long as you discover your genuine contact with Source. How will you know you have achieved this? The experience is one of feeling sacred space, of bliss, of joy. This genuine contact is experienced as quiet, which some call a still point. By some, it is simultaneously experienced as noisy, with a stream of communication coming to you from the Source, especially if you have strengthened your clairsentient, clairaudient, claircognizant, and clairvoyant abilities. These are well-developed forms of intuition, sometimes referred to as psychic abilities and sometimes referred to as "gut feelings."

I do not recall my first moment of genuine contact with Source in this lifetime. I do remember my first conscious awareness of this contact. I was nine years old, lying in my bed, mulling over some difficulties in my life. My parents had stopped talking to one another and

I could not make sense of what was going on. I only knew I was in turmoil. I prayed to ask for help. Suddenly, I was so hot I could barely stand it. I pulled the hair up off my forehead and placed my forehead against the cool plaster wall of my bedroom to cool down. Everything changed in that moment and I knew I was not alone—knew it in a profound and out-of-my-ordinary-reality way. I remember that I was not startled. I had a sense of knowing that feeling, and it was blissful. I have never lost that genuine contact with Source since then. Sometimes, when life seems to contain more difficulties than I feel I can cope with, my mind thinks I have lost the connection and I go into a mode of feeling overwhelmed. This does not last long. I find a path that works for me so that I can regain my conscious awareness of genuine contact with Source. My usual paths are to get out into nature and walk, either among the horses or on the beach with the sound of the waves and sightings of porpoises, or to look at photos of people I love. If they are nearby, even better ... I can get and give hugs and words of love, and genuine contact while Source resurfaces. I feel this genuine contact physically in the area between my throat and my heart.

I have heard people say that genuine contact with Source is mystical, as though it is attainable by only a few on this planet, by mystics. I think that the person is arguing for her limitations with this viewpoint. With a slightly expanded view from ordinary reality into non-ordinary reality, genuine contact with Source becomes quite ordinary and is indeed accessible to all of us ... very simply. The experience is not unique, and is written about in all cultures and in all traditions. Sources of inspiration include Arjuna's words in the Bhagavad Gita; writings from Celtic spirituality; teachings from shamanism from indigenous cultures around the world; Abraham; Mohammed; Buddha; Jesus; and great mystics of the creation-centered spiritual tradition, such as Hildegard of Bingen. Each of them says that you can find the way to what is sometimes referred to as illumination.

I encourage you above all to follow your heart. There is no one right way. There are, however, the works of some great teachers of the past and present within various religions, and within a greater spiritual teaching that transcends all religions.

If your path to achieving your conscious awareness of your genuine contact with Source is one of study, I encourage you to study the work of Walter Russell and his wife Lao, who started the University of Science and Philosophy. Walter Russell understood the cause of things. He was considered a heretic by the scientific community, yet in 1963 Walter Cronkite, upon Walter Russell's passing, said he was the Leonardo da Vinci of our time. Russell was accomplished in many fields, including as a scientist, philosopher, sculptor, and architect, and all this with only a fourth-grade education. He was a master of tuning in to nature and to the universal One, which was his term for God.

Note to self: return to walking my talk by getting outside in nature for an hour every day to BE with creation.

You ARE in Genuine Contact with Source

You are in genuine contact with Source. Period. You have a choice about whether you wish to be conscious of this genuine contact, explore it, and in the process expand your multidimensional awareness in this lifetime or others. I believe that conscious awareness of our genuine contact with Source happens in this lifetime regardless, yet for many people, the moment of this awareness takes place on their deathbed. You can wait until then or have a grand adventure in the exploration and accompanying expanded awareness sooner. You might even choose to begin now, and in so choosing, the adventure begins.

It is not difficult to develop your conscious awareness of your genuine contact with Source. Once upon a time, you were a newborn, and anyone who looked into your eyes as the windows to your soul could see such innocent beauty in you, and for that instant of looking, could see Source. Was this because you had so recently come from a greater awareness of who you are in relation to Source, with your messages from the angels? Making genuine contact with Source seems to be about developing your conscious awareness of something that you once knew, an act of remembering rather than developing.

I have had the exquisite experience of looking into the newborn eyes of Rachel, Laura, David, and Aaron, Jessica, and Marleigh. I could have held that gaze for an eternity with each of them; there was more beauty than can be described. The gaze went from eye to eye, heart to heart, soul to soul, and the full understanding of Source, pure love, was experienced. I can still imagine that moment with each of them and experience that exquisite sensation.

As they grew, the full understanding of genuine contact with Source seemed to recede, and yet I am sure it was not erased. This genuine contact is not difficult to achieve, because it seems to be a journey to conscious remembering what we were born having. I am not sure if what babies have in their genuine contact with Source can be called conscious awareness, and yet I believe it is conscious awareness that is simply nonverbal. Before I birthed Rachel, I read a lot of books about babies. I had never even held a baby at that point in my life, and I was desperate for information about what to do as a mother. None of the books prepared me adequately for the experience.

The information from the baby books and the experience of her conscious awareness is one example of the inadequacy of the information. As instructed in the books, I lay her down in a pram to take her for a walk. The idea was to give myself exercise and my body some help in recovering from childbirth, and to give her the fresh air and movement needed to lull her to sleep. Sleeping was something she did little of, again in contradiction to those baby books. I pushed the pram, and before long, she was crying louder and louder. Sleep was clearly not going to happen, and I took a very distraught baby back to the house. I made a few more attempts, and then had an insight. She was so aware of life that she did not want to miss anything. I sat a little infant seat inside the big pram so that she could see everything around her, and she immediately settled down.

The information about the vision of babies of that age was that they could not see so much with their physical eyes. The books did not take into account seeing with all of the other senses, and maybe with some other means of sight. With this adjustment of using the infant seat to sit her up to "see," the experience became joyful. I believe she was non-verbally and yet consciously aware of creation around her and of her connection to that creation as part of Source. Over time, as she began to speak, she was able to tell me what she saw across dimensions. At about age five this way of seeing seemed to stop, and now at thirty-one, she is remembering her way back to this conscious awareness of Source and accessing her conscious multidimensional awareness again.

When Laura came along, I did not even attempt to lay her down in a pram, and went directly to placing an infant seat in the pram so she could recline and still see. This worked well, and I was pleased with myself for my wisdom. Within two months when her neck was strong enough to move her head to look around more, this arrangement no longer worked, and I again had a baby that cried and cried whenever we got more than thirty meters along on our walk. I chose to really notice what was happening at the moment the crying would start. What I discovered was that just before the eruption of crying, her head would be turning side to side, eyes wide open.

Another mother might have concluded that she cried because what she was seeing was strange to her. My insight was that she was crying because she had so much conscious awareness that her ability to notice everything she was seeing was overwhelming her, as the filters to stop so much noticing had not yet developed. Her multisensory multidimensional awareness was in full mode and it was all just too much stimulation for her. I stopped taking her for walks and instead went by car to a park or a store to reduce the sensory experience to only one physical place. She was content and explored what she noticed with her full enthusiasm. Once her body was more mobile, she needed to touch everything, to explore not only the visuals but also the textures.

For Laura, this way of seeing Source never stopped as far as I can tell. What she did along her journey was to attempt to put this on a back burner in her conscious awareness so that she could get on with her growth. At twenty-nine, she is coming into her own as an artist, allowing herself to access her multidimensional awareness again.

David's version of his conscious awareness of Source showed up in infancy in two ways. He was very late to talk, to the point of causing his father and me some concern. We made jokes about it, watching as he made motions with his hands, which his two sisters immediately interpreted and went to meet his nonverbal requests and commands. We laughed at the time, realizing that the girls would rather do his bidding than wait until he might cry, which would disrupt their playtime. My interpretation today is that David was using his full understanding of all being connected, including multidimensionally within Source, to communicate with his sisters differently. He simply believed he would be fully understood and that his every need would be met. This aspect of his understanding of Source is something that most adults I know

Chapter Two: Health and Balance for Optimal Effectiveness

continue to strive for … the full and deep understanding that they will be fully understood and that their every need will be met by Source.

The second way his conscious awareness of multiple dimensions showed up was his demonstration of extraordinary spatial abilities very early. He somehow sees spatial aspects easily and all of the time, taking in and working with spatial dimensions of existence. A child's toy like a shape sorter was too easy for him even at nine months. As a teenager, he mastered countless fantasy video games in record time using these gifts of multidimensional sight. He takes this gift for granted, and despite being tested as having spatial abilities above ninety-eight percent of the population, he now understands that others do not have the conscious ability to perceive what is around them in the same way that he does. He uses his multidimensional abilities, at twenty-five, as a computer programmer who is able to link the needs of people with the software.

Whether it was at a gathering on our farm, or at a campground when we were camping, Aaron, as a toddler, would walk around to people who were having their meals and simply look up at them with his mouth open, assuming his need for a tasty tidbit of food would result in it being miraculously dropped into his mouth. He was connected with the energy of "doing" and trusted that his needs would be met. His connection beyond ordinary reality was evident in his communications with people and with animals. Now, you might think, what is so non-ordinary about this communication? It is similar to that of other children, absolutely. And yet it is not so ordinary to experience adults with this level of open communication and trust. Aaron, as a child, still had conscious awareness of Source. Like Rachel, his conscious awareness of his multidimensional abilities appeared hidden for some time to those around him. At twenty-four, he has remembered these abilities and he assures me that even though he didn't talk about them, he never lost them. He uses these abilities in his work as a blacksmith, imbuing his artistic pieces with specific energies based on the desire of his customers. He is also an animal communicator, with a specialty in reptiles. That is a particular cross-dimensional ability that I, as his mother, used to be a barrier to him by not letting him have snakes in the house despite his love for them!

My young grandchildren are still wide open with their genuine contact with Source and their exploration of their world. It is clear that they are communicating in all sorts of ways other than verbal communication, and that they have a lot they want to communicate about. The adults in their world are doing their best for these children to retain their conscious awareness of genuine contact with Source so that they do not go through a stage of forgetting and have to travel the long journey back to remembering this genuine contact. As a grandmother, I am noticing their genuine contact with Source, and it is beautiful.

In my university years, my undergraduate thesis was on the topic of intelligence of nonverbal preschoolers. The setting for the research study was at the preschool at the Chedoke-McMaster Hospital campus of McMaster University. My thesis director, Dr. Linda Segal, had developed an intelligence-testing machine for children who were nonverbal, and it was my job to determine whether the intelligence of a sample of nonverbal preschoolers was statistically different from the intelligence of a group of verbal preschoolers. Among the nonverbal children at this special preschool were a number of children diagnosed with autism. The intelligence test involved a machine that had screens that the children could look at and press a button if they agreed with different comparisons of pictures. For example, a series of pictures could be about opposites or similarities. When the child got a correct answer, a small candy was dispensed from the machine, and so the child, who was given no verbal instructions about what to do, figured it out based on a reward system. At the end of months of testing and applying

Chapter Two: Health and Balance for Optimal Effectiveness

the statistical formulas, there was no difference in the measured intelligence of the verbal and the nonverbal children. I have always found that result to be fascinating and wondered a lot about all the nonverbal consciousness and intelligence. I thought of these nonverbal children as being very much in genuine contact with Source, simply processing it all in non-ordinary ways.

If you want this journey of remembering your genuine contact with Source, a simple and useful starting point is to spend an hour a day out in nature, noticing what you experience and letting it communicate with you. Yes, I am suggesting something as simple as getting a chair out and sitting in the sunshine or shade, without music or anything artificial. Consider this a daily date with nature. You might prefer to lie down, to stand, or to walk. The key is to simply do it and experience your growing awareness of your genuine contact. The arts give you other ways to get in touch with Source. Read or write poetry, paint or view paintings, see a play or a movie, or create a mandala. Approach any form of art you participate in with the perspective that you will expand your conscious awareness (remembering) of your genuine contact with Source.

A key is to keep it simple and simply BE. For some of you, this may include participating in your chosen religion, and if so, this too is a good path. Again, the key is to BE and in being, to remember, rather than having someone claim that he/she is there to intercede on your behalf. You have been in a state of genuine contact with the Source from the moment you were created.

One of my favorite temples in the world is Natural Bridge in Virginia, U.S.A., about which poems have been written. Recently, I took a dear friend from India, Rajiv, to Natural Bridge. He is a devout Gandhian. As we strolled along the path, it felt like an ordinary walk until we were under the Natural Bridge. At that point, Rajiv stopped and had a more than ordinary experience of the sacredness of the place and the moment and his genuine contact with Source. What he said, when the moment was complete, was that this was as powerful as even the most magnificent of the temples in India. I agreed.

I very much enjoy and learn from the Christian teachings of Joel and Victoria Osteen, as it is uplifting and encouraging people to study the Old and New Testaments differently to understand that God wants the best for everyone and has made it possible if we only believe it is possible. I want to find a way to support them. They face a lot of criticism for their determination to teach an uplifting message.

I very much enjoy and learn from what I have studied of Gautama Buddha. Ward and I went to Sarnath in India, where Buddha gave his first sermon in relation to the suffering he was witnessing in the area of nearby Varanasi. Varanasi is a sacred place for Hindus on the Ganges River, where the cremation fires have not gone out in over 5,000 years. People flock there to die to be able to be cremated in these fires, which are said to purify the soul so it can be released from the cycle of karma. Going to the location of the first sermon put the teachings on suffering into a special perspective for us.

I very much enjoy and learn from what I have studied in Hinduism, with so many aspects of god and goddess that everything seems to be covered somewhere. Our friend Ashok told us that while it appears that different gods and goddesses are honored, they are really all aspects of the one. We had great joy going into the different temples and experiencing the feeling of the beliefs.

I very much enjoy and learn from what I have studied in the spiritual beliefs of indigenous peoples on the planet, particularly my immersion in Native American beliefs. For much of my adult life, I lived near the Six Nations Indian Reservation in Ontario, Canada, and had the opportunity for several years to work with the people in setting up their own child welfare organization on the reservation. During those

Chapter Two: Health and Balance for Optimal Effectiveness

years, I had wonderful experiences and insights from the long house tradition, along with mentoring by some of the elders.

I very much enjoy and learn from what I have studied about spiritual beliefs from metaphysical writings of wisdom from beings from other dimensions, and from studying ancient tools that tap into the metaphysical such as the Kabbalah. I note that there are a lot of metaphysical teachings in the older religions as well as from some of the most highly regarded scientists. One of my favorite teachers of the metaphysical is Dr. Toni Petrinovich in Washington, USA, and the first course I took with her was about quantum physics. She has written and has videos of teachings about metaphysics, quantum physics, spirituality, and more recently insights about "truth." She is a bridge between understanding science and spirit.

I have also learned a lot about making genuine contact with Source from movies like *Star Wars,* and books categorized as science fiction and fantasy, such as the remarkable *Dune* series by the late Frank Herbert and the *Wheel of Time* series by the late Robert Jordan, finished by Brian Sanderson.

Note to self: I look forward to experiencing other religions and beliefs that I have not yet had the privilege of immersing myself in. I look forward to further expansion and then, from this expanded state of my own being, to increased experience of genuine contact with Source. All have something to teach me, and I am committed to my growth.

Your turn.

1. If what is conveyed here is true, what would I see?
2. If what is conveyed here is true, what would I hear?
3. If what is conveyed here is true, what would I feel?
4. If what is conveyed here is true, what would I know?
5. If what is conveyed here is true, how could this affect your leadership?

Notes

CHAPTER THREE

Spirit Matters

Spirit or Conscious Energy Is All-That-Is

As you read this section, to add experiences of your own, I invite you to reflect on

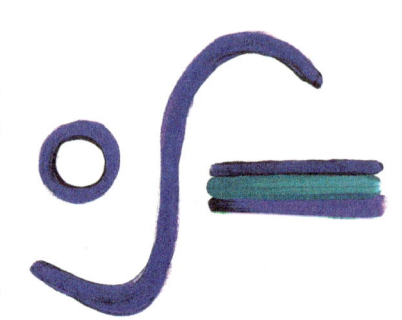

1. What color comes to mind?
2. What texture comes to mind?
3. What metaphor comes to mind?
4. What dance movement comes to mind?
5. What are you learning about genuine contact?

Faith-based people might experience Spirit as a unified field felt as the consciousness of love. Science-based people might experience Sprit by other words, possibly as a life-nurturing energy field that shows up as an oak tree out of an acorn, filled from the beginning with the life force (Spirit) of the oak tree. Others might experience Spirit as the "force," as in the *Star Wars* version of "may the force be with you." Business- or sports-minded people might experience Spirit as team spirit. It is my understanding that some winning sports teams attribute their success to meditating and being "in the zone" before a game. With our finite minds limiting our ability to grasp the infinite, Spirit might be experienced as the presence of whatever morphic fields (term created by Dr. Rupert Sheldrake, a biologist) we each choose to align ourselves with.

Chapter Three: Spirit Matters

A morphic field can be understood as a vibrational frequency or as energy in the form of a pattern of information. I believe that all of these experiences are getting at an understanding of Spirit.

A way that we as humans experience Spirit is through something we call consciousness. Increasing our consciousness or conscious energy could be experienced as increasing our conscious awareness of our oneness with Spirit. Shifting our consciousness as individuals is about getting out of our own way so that we can have more and more of this experience of Spirit for longer and longer periods of time, until we live with full and genuine recognition that Spirit or conscious energy or "the force" is all that is.

I work for Spirit, which means that I am always employed and that I am always with whoever I am meant to be with, doing exactly what I am meant to be doing, at exactly the right time, with a loving detachment toward the outcome. I am on the payroll of Spirit, with an employment contract that I have written out, which means I am never unemployed. I have also always somehow had enough to eat, shelter, and the basics of life, even at times when I worried greatly about my financial situation. In such times I would bring out my contract with Spirit and I would set worry aside and wait expectantly for what I needed to be put in place.

I believe that learning to listen to Spirit, focusing our attention on what we feel guided to focus our attention on, and taking action from the felt guidance (call it gut instinct if this helps) will achieve positive outcomes for all of humanity. Spirit is brought into matter (embodiment) by what each of us chooses to focus on in creating our personal realities, and collectively in creating our collective reality in our families, our teams, our organizations, our cities, and as a planetary collective of human beings.

I am much clearer about working with Spirit in creating my personal reality than I am about understanding how we collectively co-create without getting all entangled with each other. The best I can do at present to understand how we create the collective reality with Spirit is to explain what science calls entrainment, morphic resonance, or resonant energy fields. While science cannot explain the great mystery that is Spirit, it is very useful to draw from what science is finding to explain aspects of Spirit and how Spirit works in our lives. Through religions, humankind seeks to understand the great mystery. Along a parallel track, scientists also have sought to understand the great mystery, to understand life and what it is all about.

I had a very poignant experience in Moscow some years ago. Our friend Elena had arranged for her brother-in-law Nicoli to pick me up at the international airport, to spend the day with me, and to deliver me to the domestic airport for my flight at the end of the day to Novosibirsk. It was my first trip to Russia. I do not know what Nicoli had been told about me, but he seemed concerned that I might be religious somehow. This probably had to do with the fact that I was teaching Open Space Technology, a meeting method that has the valuable benefit, among others, that it opens space for Spirit or spirit to show up. Nicoli took me to various sites, including Red Square and the Kremlin. I asked a lot of questions and he often replied, "I don't know, I am a scientist." He was indeed a very dedicated scientist, examining life and the mystery of life through mathematical formulas.

We stopped at a rebuilt and magnificent church. It was crowded inside. There were no seats, and Nicoli left me standing in the crowd, telling me to wait and that he would be right back. In minutes, he returned with two thin tapered candles to light. He again said, "I am a scientist," and then continued with, "but since we are in a church, we will do this. Come with me and we will light our candles." We went over to a large candle lit for Mary, and we each lit our tapered candle and placed our lit candles on the altar. I do not know what Nicoli was

Chapter Three: Spirit Matters

thinking or if he said a silent prayer. I said a prayer and I also acknowledged with deep gratitude that life had allowed this precious moment for me with a Russian scientist in a church. I understood that we were both seeking to understand the same great mystery of life, each from our perceptual lens.

I do not think that science can explain religion any more than I think religion can explain science. I think that each is a path that examines who we are, why we are here, and how we are connected with our greater universe; in other words, each is a path toward working to understand what the finite mind cannot grasp ... a mystery greater than our understanding.

I have my beliefs, just as you have yours. I have my own constant relationship with the beautiful Source from which we all come and believe in the importance of prayer (talking to Source) and meditation (listening to Source). I do not want to lose you by choosing words that are contrary to your beliefs. I mean no offense, and I believe that in the end, all who pray, pray to the same Creator. We each develop different understandings, and I hope that you can read what I am saying on this subject, through the lens of your own beliefs about Spirit. Sports fans and many in business seek out spirit as in team spirit. They know that when their team is operating at the height of its potential, it is directly related to spirit. Business-, sports-, scientific- and faith-based lenses are paths to understanding that we are all somehow connected in a web of life, that there is a force, a power, a conscious energy that we can feel and cannot measure. We can measure some of the tangible outcomes of working with this force, but the force itself is beyond measurement.

In my experience, Spirit flows through us, to us, all around us, and is all that is. When I experience Spirit working with me, I experience access to knowledge, creativity, compassion, and the field of all possibilities. I experience an all-pervasive conscious energy working through me and in me. I believe it is there all the time. However, I am more conscious of it when I am willing and open to embrace the power within me and when I am taking active steps, even if only baby steps, to move forward with my life. I discover a lot of synchronicities that of course I find interesting, and sometimes there are so many in a short span of time that I can feel overwhelmed in my joy. In my awareness that Sprit is all that is, I experience many miracles.

My friends who speak German and French have told me that there is not an easy way to translate this concept of Spirit into their languages. If you are uncomfortable with the word Spirit or even spirit, or if this word doesn't translate well for you in your primary language, perhaps Conscious Energy is a way to describe what I call Spirit that will resonate with you. How Spirit, Source, Conscious Energy came to BE is part of the great mystery. I experience this energy as conscious, as love, as joy, as compassion, as creativity, and it "in-spires" me. In-spire is spirit or Spirit within. I believe that joy is my birthright, and when I am in joy, I am in my truest, purest alignment with the vibration frequency of this Conscious Energy. I choose, for the purpose of this book, to refer to both Spirit and Creator as Source, and I am hoping that you can find your own way to substitute your preferred word and accompanying beliefs. There is no one right way.

Note to self: some people are fascinated by Spirit in business and the concept of spiritual intelligence as a business asset. Others have cautioned me not to write about Spirit, as it will turn so many people away from interest in this book. I think it is important to stand behind sharing my experiences and perceptions so that those who follow this work can make up their own minds about what they want to believe. I can hear friends saying, "Birgitt, when you talk about Spirit, your important and useful work stops being accessible to people." I am answering, "When I talk about Spirit, and encourage people to make their own choices, I am making my work accessible to people who want to either accept or reject what I am saying, because I am creating conditions for personal wisdom to emerge."

Matters of Spirit and of Science

In my studies, I have come to believe that both science and religion have the goal of explaining the great mystery of the universe, creation, and our source, whether examining something microscopic or macroscopic. I am intrigued by the overlaps that I read about from these two different dimensions of exploring what I think of as our omniverse. Both seek to understand what I choose to call Spirit. I believe that spiritual principles transcend all religions and all science as we currently know it. Mind is immaterial and not subject to the universal laws of matter that scientists have studied. Mind, which is not understood as having a beginning or an end, is not subject to the laws of science or religion, but is subject to spiritual laws. If mind is one dimension of consciousness, or conscious energy, then consciousness is also subject to spiritual laws.

Jesus was the most scientific man to have ever trod the globe, according to Mary Baker Eddy in her writings of 1875. He taught us about what we now call quantum physics, about particles, waves, and how to achieve miracles. He also told us that what he did could be done by all of us. In our times, a person who has done extensive research on the physics of miracles and is offering something very useful to humanity is Dr. Richard Bartlett. He is teaching his audiences how to use what is known in quantum physics as "collapsing a wave" to achieve some miraculous results. When I was in the audience and learning from him, what appeared to be done seemed very similar to what Jesus did. In collapsing the wave, Dr. Bartlett accesses what scientists refer to as the zero-point energy field. I think of this field as a state of Divine Grace and the moment of accessing this phenomenal energy as a sacred moment. (Remember that this is me sharing with you my perspective from my beliefs.)

It takes more than knowledge of quantum physics to do what Dr. Bartlett does and what people in his audiences discover they can do too. It takes an understanding of the difference between feelings and the feeling state, how to move beyond feelings into the feeling state of love or the sacred, and from that feeling state, to achieve a non-ordinary reality that is the reality of what some would call miracles. Dr. Bartlett and others are currently exploring non-ordinary reality through a combination of science and spirituality or mysticism. Again, the theme of great theoretical physicists having become mystics is showing up.

Science

I am reading Ken Wilber's *Quantum Questions* as I search for the parallel journeys of theoretical physics and mysticism.[10] If I understand Ken Wilber correctly, he cautions his audience not to attempt to use science to explain the mystical, and that they are

Chapter Three: Spirit Matters

simply two different streams of knowledge that look at the same thing from different perspectives. I am a student of science and I am a student of spirituality.

As a professional organizational development consultant, I get enjoyment in exploring my world from the perspective of how my learning applies to organizations. Many organizational development theorists use quantum physics and chaos theories to explain how organizational development should be done. I am not sure that applying these theories to organizational development will prove useful if it is true that Spirit is all that is. I suppose that this depends on the interpretation of what Spirit is and whether Spirit is simply a neutral zero-point energy, a creative life force energy, or an energy that can best be felt as the energy field of Divine Grace or love.

I am also respectful of theories as being simply beliefs to be proven, and then generally discounted at some later point in our evolution when other theories are proven more correct. History shows us that great revelations of science are ultimately transcended by something else. In organizational development and other practices that like to borrow scientific theories, I think it is most useful if we don't take them too seriously but learn to play rather than believing that the theories are the truth, the whole truth, and nothing but the truth. Playing allows us to stay open to the sea of possibilities.

I believe that a great disservice was done to humanity when science and religion were separated, and wonder what theories might have been created if the two had remained in union. Today, we experience many people being quite negative about astrology, saying it is too much of a soft science or too esoteric. Those same people might admire astronomy because they admire only what they refer to as hard science. Yet, once upon a time, astronomy and astrology were united as one science. Would we have been wiser if divisions such as this had not occurred?

Note to self: I love soft science. In my current understanding of how my brain works, the left hemisphere of my brain, the linear processor, loves hard science that is easily measurable, and the right hemisphere of my brain, the parallel processor, loves to play in possibility thinking. I wonder if I can do what Dr. Bartlett suggests and give my left hemisphere something to measure so that my right hemisphere can be more creative. I intend to experiment with this.

Your turn.

1. If what is conveyed here is true, what would I see?
2. If what is conveyed here is true, what would I hear?
3. If what is conveyed here is true, what would I feel?
4. If what is conveyed here is true, what would I know?
5. If what is conveyed here is true, how could this affect your leadership?

Notes

Theoretical Physics

As you read this segment, to add experiences of your own, I invite you to reflect on

1. What color comes to mind?
2. What texture comes to mind?
3. What metaphor comes to mind?
4. What dance movement comes to mind?
5. What are you learning about genuine contact?

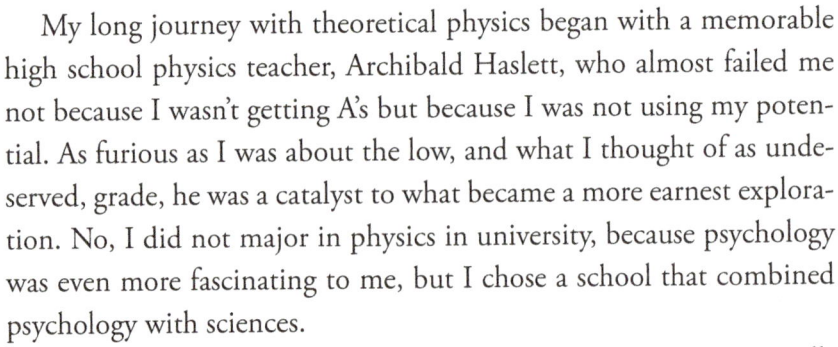

My long journey with theoretical physics began with a memorable high school physics teacher, Archibald Haslett, who almost failed me not because I wasn't getting A's but because I was not using my potential. As furious as I was about the low, and what I thought of as undeserved, grade, he was a catalyst to what became a more earnest exploration. No, I did not major in physics in university, because psychology was even more fascinating to me, but I chose a school that combined psychology with sciences.

In my second year, along with an entire class of students, I sat spellbound every Monday, Wednesday, and Friday mornings at eight a.m. It is difficult to imagine university students being spellbound at that hour of the morning, and yet, there we were, early for the class, pens poised in readiness, waiting for Professor Brown to make his punctual appearance. The class was Time and Space, and in it we were introduced to concepts like past, present, and future all existing simultaneously. We were introduced to the great theoretical physicists and their work; we were introduced to string theory, Schrödinger's experiment, quantum physics, and chaos theory. If you do not have a class like that in your area and you are interested in these topics, groups like Scientific American take complex theories such as explaining the universe and how creation seems to work, and simplify these bewildering ideas for the public to facilitate understanding. Groups like the Institute of Noetic Sciences do the same in explaining consciousness, providing theories and information that is truly extraordinary.

I have been most fascinated by Einstein, the scientist and the mystic, who was involved in a long search for a unified theory. He searched for a single set of equations that could incorporate both relativity and quantum mechanics, combining the macro-level physics of stars and galaxies with the laws of the microlevel subatomic realm. He struggled with this quest from the 1920s until his death in 1955, and the degree of success that he had is questionable. Einstein was simply ahead of his time. More than half a century later, his dream of a unified field theory has become the Holy Grail of modern physics. From my perspective, all this research gives us a window to look at Spirit where we would find the unity of connectedness beyond even a unified field theory.

There is quantum mechanics, which is the branch of physics that deals with the study of particles down to the atomic and subatomic level. Energy is perceived to be in the form of quanta (or small packets). When we get down to the level of looking at energy, I think we get closer to looking at Spirit, because Spirit can be experienced as conscious energy. I am not so sure about the packets, though. Quantum mechanics does allow scientists to think of interactions between correlated objects that move faster than the speed of light, which was quite a breakthrough. A concept first proposed by Einstein and colleagues is that all quantum mechanical systems have a ground state, which they referred to as zero-point energy, the lowest possible energy that a quantum mechanical system could have. From zero-point energy came the zero-point energy field, the quantum mechanical system that encapsulates this zero-point energy. Zero-point energy is sometimes thought of as empty space.

There is string theory and research looking at whether string theory could be the elegant explanation of everything. I think Professor Brown would be pointing students to search http://www.pbs.org/wgbh/nova/elegant just to expand their perspectives. The website has some easy-to-understand diagrams and includes information about eleven dimensions, parallel universes, and a world made out of strings. It is not science fiction. It seems to be one aspect of understanding the omniverse.

Chaos theory describes reality as apparently disordered, yet there is actually order underlying this appearance. One way I came to understand more was through James Gleick's book, *Chaos: Making a New Science,* thankfully written in an interesting way for beginners.[11] The usual example given of chaos theory is about the flapping of a single butterfly's wing producing a tiny change in the state of the atmosphere. This same tiny action with minimal apparent impact on the atmosphere could be responsible for a tornado in a month's time, or it could be responsible for stopping such a tornado. What happens from the flapping of the wings depends on the initial conditions within which the butterfly flapped its wings. Chaos theory seems to be another aspect of understanding the omniverse.

I think that all these theories are taking us closer and closer to understanding that Spirit or conscious energy is all that is. I recognize that I may not understand the zero-point field enough, because somewhere I have read that this zero-point field is the lowest energy and that its ground state is non-zero, which to me means there is energy

Chapter Three: Spirit Matters

there. That may be it. If energy is there, and if science is not measuring what is truly there, scientists may simply not yet have understood that they need to look for love and the sacred, and that Spirit is all that is. If conscious energy is all that is, it is conscious and thus more like a field of love or the sacred than it is a zero-point energy. Is it possible, without getting into religious interpretations of Spirit, that Spirit is a fundamental building block of everything?

In both physics and chemistry, wave-particle duality is a concept of quantum mechanics which notes that all energy exhibits both particle-like and wavelike properties. Apparently, if particles are too small for scientists to be able to see the wave, the theory has it that the wave still exists. At least this is what leading scientists have proposed in response to an age-old debate about light and matter in which one side of the debate was that light was made up of waves, while the other side was that light was made up of particles. For most of us, it doesn't matter whether light is made up of waves or particles; it only matters that we can use it to see our way in the dark. Similarly, I believe Spirit is all that is, not wondering so much about *what* Spirit is but *how* to work with Spirit for life on this planet to evolve in ways that nurture the beings of the planet and the planet herself.

Still, the scientific journey of examining "what is" is fascinating. To compound the interesting theories, which have been substantiated by mathematical formulas—likely at some point to be superseded by other theories, also substantiated by mathematical formulas—there is the factor of how this unfolding data is measured. According to Einstein in his thought experiments, thought is the tool for measurement. According to John von Neumann, the act of observing collapses the possible into what is then measured as the actual. Dr. Richard Bartlett in his *Physics of Miracles* reminds us that what we focus on is a pattern of information that shows up as matter.[12] When we change our point of focus, we pay attention to a different pattern of information, and in that moment, we might be accessing a different dimension of what we call reality with equal validity in what gets measured. I think he would be saying that if one scientist focuses on zero-point energy, she will be able to ascertain that this is reality. If I focus on Spirit is all that is, I will be able to ascertain that this is reality.

A recent personal example of reality shifting based on what I focused on was in the dentist's chair. Ever since I was a small child where our dentist had the nickname "the butcher," I have had anxiety about being in the dentist's chair. We have a wonderful holistic dentist now, and yet the old anxiety that has no reason for being in my present reality still shows up. My dental visit was simply for a cleaning and for the usual bi-yearly x-rays. I intensely dislike the plastic pieces that I have to bite down on when the technician takes the x-ray, especially the ones furthest back in my mouth that cause me to have a gag reflex. On this particular visit, I had a different technician. As she put the plastic piece into the back of my mouth, she instructed me to raise my leg up off the chair and hold my foot up during the x-ray. I did as instructed. She came back in and smilingly asked me if my gag reflex had been activated during the process. I assured her that, much to my amazement, it had not. She laughed and said that it is a little trick that she uses from her knowledge of "what you focus on becomes your reality." I had focused on my foot and forgotten all about the uncomfortable plastic in my mouth. This simple trick shifted my reality for the moment, taking me into a different dimension of my consciousness.

All of this leads me to wonder about the various theories, the role of the observer, the role of focus, and whether we truly know what our universe or the omniverse is made up of, even if hard science proves something. Yet I think that science has given us some keys for understanding HOW to work with Spirit even if it hasn't explained what Spirit is.

Chapter Three: Spirit Matters

Note to self: again, I am finding words limiting and possibly getting in the way of communication. I can just as easily say Spirit is all that is or Conscious Energy is all that is. It means the same to me. I cannot say "energy is all that is" because this creates a picture in my mind of energy as being unconscious. I believe energy to be conscious.

Your turn.

1. If what is conveyed here is true, what would I see?
2. If what is conveyed here is true, what would I hear?
3. If what is conveyed here is true, what would I feel?
4. If what is conveyed here is true, what would I know?
5. If what is conveyed here is true, how could this affect your leadership?

Notes

Entrainment

As you read this segment, to add experiences of your own, I invite you to reflect on

1. What color comes to mind?
2. What texture comes to mind?
3. What metaphor comes to mind?
4. What dance movement comes to mind?
5. What are you learning about genuine contact?

One of Ward's first gifts to me was Bentov's book *Stalking the Wild Pendulum*.[13] I could not put it down as I grasped the importance of the topic of entrainment. I was making a connection between what some call synchronicity with entrainment. Examples of entrainment are Rachel and I phoning each other at the same time; Ward and I answering a question the same way at the same time; Laura and I having the same thought at the same time; and Laura telling me something she is concerned about for Aaron at the exact moment that Aaron is sending an email asking the question. It is fascinating to track this type of entrainment, tracking the frequency in my own life of examples of the calibration of two people's thoughts.

Entrainment occurs physically too. The most commonly stated example is that when women live together in a house, after a time, the monthly cycle of each woman is on the same dates. I don't know which of the original monthly cycles win out as the dominant force to which the others entrain. Another example of entrainment is an often-told example of monkeys on an island somewhere, with a few of them washing potatoes before they eat them. This story has so many variations that I am not sure if it begins with one monkey and shifts to a few, or begins with a few. I am also not sure if it is potatoes or some other kind of vegetable or fruit. And I am not sure of the location of the island. The point can be made without all of this being known. Some monkeys started washing potatoes before they ate them. Then other monkeys on the island joined in and also washed their potatoes. Before long, all monkeys on the island were entrained in the same behavior. This was remarkable enough. Even more remarkable was that monkeys on nearby islands who had not seen this potato-washing behavior also started to wash their potatoes before eating them.

The influence of entrainment appears to be very powerful. Yet until I read *Stalking the Wild Pendulum*, I had not encountered the concept. It is not a concept that I have found to be generally discussed as a topic worth noting. I have not noticed it as a significant topic in organizational development literature, although there is talk of a tipping point and a Critical Mass theory that postulates that when a critical mass of people have agreed to something, others start aligning to it. I encourage you to pay attention to the concept of entrainment and its effect on your life. You are likely to be aligning yourself, through entrainment, with energy fields in ways that you are not aware of. You might have aligned yourself to energy fields that are not good for your well-being and you might not even be conscious of having done so.

A key experiment in *Stalking the Wild Pendulum* that led to the title of the book involves old-style pendulum clocks. The scientists involved had a wall full of these pendulum clocks. You might not know what a pendulum clock is, so I'll explain a little. Pendulum clocks have a clock face with hands that go around pointing to the numbers to show the time. They have a pendulum underneath the clock face that swings back and forth as the way of keeping time and moving the hands on the clock, and it is possible to hear this as some type of tick-tock sound. In this study, almost all of the pendulums were swinging at slightly different times, not synchronized with each other. A couple of the pendulums were in synch with the others. Apparently overnight, as witnessed by the scientists in the morning, all of the clocks on the wall entrained to each other's rhythm and all pendulums (without exception) were moving in synch with each other. There had been no interference from humans. The pendulums all adjusted their rhythm and entrained to the dominant pattern. The dominant pattern is referred to as a resonant energy field generator, generating an electromagnetic frequency. The particular electromagnetic frequency is a vibrational field.

I have witnessed this entrainment time and again in workplaces. Executive team members and the human resources department work hard and expend a great amount of resources to hire exactly the right person for a vacant position. The criteria to be met are to find someone who is productive, innovative, creative, efficient, and has demonstrated leadership skills. The team is in dire need of someone to get a team that is in a slump moving again. After being in the position for three months, the person is behaving exactly like the rest of the team. The executives and the human resources people are wondering what happened, because they had been so careful in the hiring process. I observe the effects of entrainment to the dominant vibrational field around me all the time.

I think advertisers on television and online work with this concept of entrainment. It seems that people do not know that the advertisers are deliberately creating a resonant energy field and that they know how to use this to achieve entrainment with a product. The effects of vibrational frequency on what the human does are natural. What

Chapter Three: Spirit Matters

is frightening is that humans seem to be easily manipulated by the entrainment factor to fields of vibration that on some unconscious energy level a person has aligned herself with.

As I mentioned before, morphic field is a term introduced by biologist Rupert Sheldrake to describe behaviors of species that align themselves to a vibrational field. A morphic field can be understood as a vibrational frequency or as energy in the form of a pattern of information. Sheldrake's studies were extrapolated from earlier biologists who identified morphogenetic fields of cells. Anything that you can name has a morphic field. Whether others entrain to that morphic field depends on how strong the morphic field (vibrational field, energetic pattern of information) is as a resonant energy generator. Very powerful people such as Mahatma Gandhi or Socrates were very strong resonant energy field generators, emitting strong morphic fields to which others aligned.

I like being conscious about morphic fields, entrainment, and resonant energy field generators. The reason I like being conscious of the vibrational energy fields is that it is possible to align myself, to allow entrainment, with morphic fields that I see benefit in entraining myself with. By entraining myself to the morphic field, I have access to the information in that morphic field. You can actually choose to do this too if you believe doing so will benefit your life. I have consciously aligned myself with a number of morphic fields and can access information from those morphic fields. My choices have included the morphic fields of the Christ consciousness, Buddha consciousness, Yogananda, Sai Baba, Mother Mary, Mary Magdalene, Miracles, the Genuine Contact Way, of joyful marriage, of a benevolent Source, Mother, Teacher, Healer, within me is the blueprint for my optimal health, the Order of Michael, the Order of Brigid, Matrix Energetics, Awakened Wellness, Joel and Victoria Osteen's teachings, and I will have abundance always. Yes, every one of those is a morphic field to which I have aligned myself, and my life has been deeply enriched as a result. In choosing alignment, I do not need to know anything about it in order to access the benefits of the pattern of information in the morphic field.

Some of them are archetypes, designating them as patterns of information that Carl Jung said were within the knowledge of all of us on the planet. Morphic fields have cumulative memory. The more people who align with a morphic field, the stronger the field becomes as a resonant energy generator attractor and as accessible information. The good news is that you, like me, can derive great benefit from the gateway to a pattern of information by making conscious choices of the morphic fields you choose to align yourself with. This includes the morphic fields of I am powerful, I am beautiful, I am wealthy, I am giving, I am compassionate, and so on. I encourage you to choose a morphic field to consciously align to and explore what happens. If you align to the morphic field of miracles, don't be surprised if you experience more and more miracles in your daily life.

You might have unconsciously aligned yourself with morphic fields that are not nurturing for your well-being. A morphic field that I am witnessing countless numbers of people in North America align themselves to is that of "needing pharmaceutical drugs." This has been achieved by so much advertising on television, at least three times an hour on every channel, advising people that they have symptoms that need to be treated with a drug. I could say it is like brainwashing. Yet, this is only one aspect of what is happening. A morphic field, an energetic pattern of information, a vibrational field has been created by the pharmaceutical companies to achieve entrainment. Sadly, with people unaware that they are aligning themselves to morphic fields, they are aligning anyway, albeit unconsciously.

Chapter Three: Spirit Matters

I encourage you to develop awareness that you can choose not to be in a relationship with a problem. If you choose to be in a relationship with a problem, that then becomes the field you are resonating with, based on entrainment within a resonant energy field. As an organizational consultant, I have collected interesting data over the years about people aligning themselves to the morphic field of problems. I worked with a university in 2002 which was in a situation of immobility as a faculty due to conflicts. When asked when the problem started, I was told 1908. I looked around and I knew that none of the people had been around at the start of the problem, as they were not old enough. So how did a problem that was a hotly debated issue in 1908 become such an expensive issue for the university in 2002? The people along the way had created a relationship with a problem through a morphic field about the problem. They had allowed themselves to become aligned to the morphic field of the original problem without even realizing it. They were surprised to discover the root of their present-day conflicts.

In another situation, in working with a government department of about six hundred persons, we found the same type of situation. The quality of public service of this department was so poor that it made newspaper headlines. The leaders engaged our services, having worked at fixing the situation for about six years with no gains having been made. In fact, the opposite was happening. Numbers of new staff were in place, and at about three months into the job, they were completely enmeshed in behaviors of poor performance, complaint, and a sense of victimhood. Sometimes when we see these results, we discover that the conditions for the employees to work in are so life-depleting that our work focuses on the conditions. In this situation, the conditions were excellent, and the leadership team was doing all the right things to bring about improved worker happiness and performance, yet they were not successful. The leadership team before them had also not been successful.

We discovered that in 1979 there had been a serious problem with incompetent and punitive leadership that had almost led to strike action by the workforce. Thirty years ago, emotions were deeply engaged in a situation, there were fights, conflicts, and a one-day walkout that was highly publicized. Only five of the six hundred staff members were present thirty years ago when the problems began. However, the morphic field of the problem was strong, and during the following thirty years, almost every new staff member developed a relationship with the original situation and thus aligned with the morphic field of the problem. In the present time, this problem did not exist. Energetically, it continued to exist across time because of the alignment to the morphic field. The way out of that mess was to develop a strong resonant energy generation to a different morphic field and simultaneously to assist people in becoming conscious of their alignment to the morphic field of the problem. They were surprised at their discoveries.

Dr. Bruce Lipton has done groundbreaking work with the biology of beliefs, work that can be understood best from his various YouTube videos.[14] For example, according to his work, just because a person's mother and grandmother both died from ovarian cancer at age fifty, it does not mean that the person will have the same fate. It is apparently not in the genes but in the belief system. My understanding of Dr. Lipton's research is that the reason the person would also get cancer is because she believes this to be true, and her beliefs trigger certain physiological responses. In other words, the person lines up with the morphic field of the pattern of information of "every woman in our family dies of cancer at age fifty."

Are beliefs that strong in defining our reality? I think our best scientists are discovering this to be true. We have a friend whose father died at age fifty-four from a heart attack, as did our friend's older brother. Our friend has so firmly believed that he will also die at about the same age that he is constructing his whole life to achieve this outcome. We are watching as he sabotages his life, holds firmly to the belief of an oncoming heart attack, and refuses to change his diet or to exercise. It is like watching a story unfold whose ending is already known. He has aligned with the morphic field of "I am going to get a heart attack and die before I am sixty."

By choosing the morphic fields that you align yourself with, you are making choices of either imprisoning yourself or empowering yourself. How are you letting entrainment affect you? What morphic fields have you aligned yourself with? Discerning the morphic fields you have aligned yourself with may be very useful in getting the results you want in your life. You might benefit from making more conscious choices regarding entrainment and morphic fields and how your life aligns with various vibrational fields. What does this information about entrainment and morphic fields and people as resonant energy field generators have to do with Spirit is all that is?

Some people, through meditation, prayer, and their faith have gateways to working with Spirit. For others, concepts such as entrainment and morphic fields may be easier gateways to work from. Some people may be comfortable believing that Spirit is all that is. Others will be more comfortable acknowledging that conscious energy is all that is. It is helpful to shift from thinking of energy in terms of positive and negative particles and to start thinking of energy as conscious energy. It is helpful to understand that if Spirit is all that is, or conscious energy is all that is, then you are also part of the big sea of Spirit or conscious energy. It is useful to figure out what the impact of remaining unconscious about conscious energy is having on your life.

How do you know if a particular morphic field is right for who you are? Only you can know through how it makes you feel when you align with the morphic field. Do you feel resonance with that field? Do you feel harmonious with that field? Or does alignment with that morphic field cause a feeling of disruption or discord? Your feeling center is at your heart center. Once you are consciously choosing what you align yourself with, it is important to learn to stay in touch with your heart, with your feeling center. It is a valuable source of information for your "self-guidance system."

Note to self: I think of some children's television shows about morphing into superheroes to save the day. I think the one that my children used to watch was called *Power Rangers*. The Power Rangers morphed from ordinary reality into superhero non-ordinary reality. I am now seeing this as aligning first with one morphic field and then with another morphic field, and I am thinking how cleverly these concepts are being taught. I think it is helpful to adults to watch children imagine what it is to morph and to play as though the new alignment is reality.

Your turn.

1. If what is conveyed here is true, what would I see?
2. If what is conveyed here is true, what would I hear?
3. If what is conveyed here is true, what would I feel?
4. If what is conveyed here is true, what would I know?
5. If what is conveyed here is true, how could this affect your leadership?

Notes

Working with the Morphic Field, with Spirit, with Conscious Energy

As you read this segment, to add experiences of your own, I invite you to reflect on

1. What color comes to mind?
2. What texture comes to mind?
3. What metaphor comes to mind?
4. What dance movement comes to mind?
5. What are you learning about genuine contact?

Whatever ways work for you to work with Spirit is what is right for you. Perhaps you pray, meditate, or take action in other ways. Perhaps you work with Spirit through what your religion teaches you, or what you have discerned for yourself. Perhaps you work with Spirit through the teachings of Abraham about the Law of Attraction. Perhaps you work with Spirit without agreeing that Spirit exists, and instead you refer to Spirit as the force, the flow, or another name. I do not think the name you use matters, as long as you believe that this life force energy is conscious energy. I choose to believe that Spirit is a life-force-nurturing energy, and this has been my experience of Spirit. Based on information about morphic fields, it's possible that my experience is based on my beliefs and the patterns of information that I have chosen to align myself with.

Chapter Three: Spirit Matters

Because I believe that Spirit is a life-force-nurturing energy, my knowledge of how to work with Spirit is in alignment with my belief. I have no interest in beliefs of Spirit as punitive or destructive, with the certainty that people who align themselves with such beliefs will also have the experience that goes along with the pattern of information that they align themselves to. If by chance you have unconsciously aligned yourself to a pattern of information, it is time to discover what you are aligned to and to decide if you want to make any adjustments.

Working with Spirit requires me to go out of my comfort zone a lot. Just when I am getting settled into a comfort zone of ordinary reality, I get surprised. The surprise usually results in me expanding my perspective of what is real. I end up with a new comfort zone that includes the expanded perspective. I then get settled into my new ordinary reality. And guess what? I get surprised again. The process of expansion continues, and I realize that in working with Spirit, it is important to recognize that expansion and growth are constant. You will find that you leave behind any sense of a singular ordinary reality and that you shift your consciousness into what is currently perceived by you as non-ordinary reality.

Non-ordinary reality for me has required that I get used to reality as multidimensional, including the presence of beings in other dimensions. For instance, I believe in a dimension where we exist in between lives. I believe in a dimension within which angels exist, including our specific guardian angels. I believe in other beings in other dimensions, some of whom work through mediums and gifted intuitives (sometimes called psychics) to communicate with us. I am most interested in those who communicate with us to help us work toward the best possible future. I find it useful to have sessions with people who are gifted in direct and clear interdimensional communication so that I can make better informed decisions about my personal life and my business. I also learn from other dimensional beings through books and tapes that are available. I am a fan of Esther and Jerry Hicks' work in disseminating the information from the being known as Abraham. In the Law of Attraction, Abraham teaches a lot about how to work with Spirit.

When I taught my children about working with Spirit, I followed the advice given by Abraham. The advice includes: 1. making an intention, 2. letting go of attachment to outcome, and then, 3. shifting consciousness to be in a state of allowing Spirit to do the work of Spirit. Staying in this state is simply waiting with expectancy without attachment to a particular outcome, knowing that the results will be beneficial. Richard Bartlett has wonderful advice for doing this. He gives the left hemisphere of the brain, which is the linear processor, something to do. For instance, the left hemisphere of the brain loves to measure. Having the left hemisphere measure the starting point and measure the desired outcome is giving it something that it loves to do. This then allows the right hemisphere, the parallel processor, to stay open for what comes out of the many possibilities. His description of doing this is very useful in how to state the intention and then get out of the way, especially getting the linear processor of the brain out of the way, or else it keeps wanting to measure whether the result has happened or not. Measurement is not in the physical body; it is in thought.

I have taught my children that Spirit requires that they also do some of the work, and that sitting back and simply creating a wish list of intentions is not how to work with Spirit. When they have been in distress of some type, I have them write their intentions down on index cards, one intention per card. The next part of the task I give them is to figure out any and all actions that they might take to achieve their intention, including both small actions and bigger ones, writing each one on a separate index card. When all of the ideas have been generated, every intention has a number of actions associated with it.

Chapter Three: Spirit Matters

I advise that every day, there should be some progress on one of the action steps, even if only a teeny-tiny one, to demonstrate working with Spirit in positive expectancy.

In working with Spirit, I get myself out of my lens of habitual perception of my ordinary reality. I choose to stay open to the non-ordinary, to the surprise, to the miracles. By getting myself out of my lens of habitual perception, I pay attention to what shows up. This can be a lot of fun. I am convinced that Spirit is a conscious energy with a great sense of humor. I have walked through a bookstore, contemplating a question, and had a book fall right off the shelf onto the floor in front of me. I notice and then discover that what is in the book is the answer to my question. If I had not been noticing, I would not be open to taking a look at the book that fell off the shelf, because the logical part of my brain would have come up with a rational concept of why the book had fallen. The non-logical part of my brain that wants to play would notice the book and engage with it to find out what gift it had brought me.

Once when I was facilitating a community meeting, a woman came up to me at the break. She said that she had no interest in the community meeting but had come specifically to talk to me. I waited to find out what she wanted to know, which was a bit egotistical. She didn't want anything at all from me, but wanted to give me a tip. I paid attention, because this was clearly not what I was expecting, and so I noticed that there was something different. She then said that she had just read a book called *Molecules of Emotion*, and that she felt inspired to come and relay the information about this book to me because it would be important for me.[15] End of conversation as she moved away. I bought the book and it indeed was important to something I was seeking at that time. My job was to be open to what non-ordinary reality presented to me, to notice.

I think that the word "in-spiring" is worthy of extra notice. It implies the work of Spirit as spirit within. One way that I experience working with Spirit when I have figured something out is that I end up with a feeling of "aha." When I want to expand my perceptual field to find solutions, I let go of thought, emotions, outcome, and go within. As I feel in-spired, I know that Spirit worked with me to guide me to the solution.

I cannot access this state when I am stressed. I usually go into flight mode rather than fight mode when I am stressed, but when I am in either mode, I am so tense that I cannot go to this internal still point to be in-spired. I have a number of ways that I have found to destress myself so that I can work with Spirit. Every morning, I do a form of tai chi called Y-Dan, immediately followed by Peter Van Daam's yoga, which was designed from the teachings of Edgar Cayce. Both work every vertebra and exercise every organ. Exercises to draw the shoulders up and drop them down are included, and I can feel the stress leave with these exercises in particular. I destress with favorite activities and hobbies. I destress when I am sitting in a rocking chair on our front porch watching and noticing the nature all around me. I destress when I am with people I love, cooking together, laughing together, even working together.

I have a Freeze-Framer software program from the HeartMath Institute that I use to measure my ability to have heart with brain coherence, a state that is free of stress. It is a great biofeedback device so that I can learn more about when I am feeling stress and when I am not. By noticing what no stress feels like, I can return to the state of no stress more easily. I want to be in the shape I need to be in to listen to Spirit working in me.

I expect miracles and I love miracles. I express my gratitude for the miracles every day, sometimes in the morning, sometimes again

Chapter Three: Spirit Matters

at night, and sometimes as they are unfolding. What has happened is that so many occur that I cannot keep up with my expressions of gratitude. While on this subject of miracles, I want to draw your attention back to morphic fields and entrainment again. When I align myself with miracles, and others align themselves with miracles, is it possible that we are programming the consciousness of miracles into a morphic field for humanity at this time. And if this is true, might there be entrainment of humanity to miracles? And if this is true, what might this mean for the future of humanity? To work with Spirit, it is useful to use your imagination. There are infinite possibilities of what can be created.

Note to self: if Spirit is all that is, and what we see as reality is Spirit as matter, then we must be working with Spirit all the time. I think what I have been writing about is developing conscious awareness of working with Spirit so that I am more of a co-creator of my future. John Pothiah, a gifted clairsentient that I go to for guidance from time to time, has taught me about destiny markers, karma, and free will as three aspects that influence my future. I think my writing was about the free will aspect. Destiny markers are the Divine Plan for me within which I use my free will. The people and circumstances I deal with and need to learn from are influenced by karma. Working with Spirit is a big subject.

Your turn.

1. If what is conveyed here is true, what would I see?
2. If what is conveyed here is true, what would I hear?
3. If what is conveyed here is true, what would I feel?
4. If what is conveyed here is true, what would I know?
5. If what is conveyed here is true, how could this affect your leadership?

Notes

CHAPTER FOUR

Change Is Constant

I Believe that Change with Its Accompanying Loss, Grief Work, and Conflict Is Constant

Individuals and organizations that develop mastery in working with change can sustain optimal effectiveness. These leaders and organizations recognize that change cannot be managed, that energy spent trying to manage change is wasted energy, and that productive use of individual and organizational energy is achieved by working with change rather than against it.

As you read this segment, to add experiences of your own, I invite you to reflect on

1. What color comes to mind?
2. What texture comes to mind?
3. What metaphor comes to mind?
4. What dance movement comes to mind?
5. What are you learning about genuine contact?

Chapter Four: Change Is Constant

Life surges. There seems to be something intangible behind the life we see, a life force. Scientists, theologians, ancient and modern mystics all have their explanations. I understand that it is a great mystery and that our minds, at this point in our evolution, may not be capable of understanding the answer. I have created some belief patterns that are useful to me in leading my life. I encourage you to do the same. I hope that when many of us are seeking a life-nurturing future for all, we can indeed have significant influence on the future individually, organizationally, and globally. I hope that we can create a shift in consciousness away from fear and a sense of victimhood, to empowered co-creating.

I choose to believe that life force is a creative rather than a destructive force. To thrive in constant change as individuals and as organizations, I think it is useful to flow with this life force. I think it is useful to have mastery in influencing this life force to the fullest extent that we have influence.

If you have found ways to stay in the flow with life force, you have already developed some of the mastery you need for thriving in change. I have many experiences of struggling against it. I do not know why I chose to create a lot of my experiences by struggling against this life force that I think of as Spirit, but I did. In my struggle, I would run into a gentle barrier, which I could have heeded and gotten back into the flow. I often did not do so, and then ran into a larger barrier, which was not so gentle. Because I have a tendency to persevere, what some might call stubbornness, I would continue struggling and attempting to control the way that I wanted my life to go. I can attest to the struggle ending in painful experiences. I thought of some of these painful experiences as being hit in the head by a block of wood. Only then would I stop, reassess, and figure out where the life flow was taking me. In more recent years, I have made a conscious effort to learn how to correct my course back into this flow at the first sign of gentle nudges. I do not want to invite the "block of wood in the head" experience. I continue working on developing my mastery of staying in the flow.

If you have found ways to influence this life force where it can be influenced, you have already developed some of the mastery you need for thriving in change. In our unfolding story as humans, we have ample evidence of the power of prayer, the power of intention, and the power of even a single individual having profound and widespread influence. A very gifted psychic that I admire, John Pothiah in Ontario, Canada, a true clairsentient communicator, has guided me in understanding that the flow of our lives is affected by destiny markers, by karma, and by free will. I believe that my oversoul has to come to some sort of agreement with the destiny markers and karma that affect my life for the purpose of the particular experiences I need for my growth and expansion in this lifetime. My oversoul has, through free will, made choices and contracts that affect my life. Nothing is there to punish me or to reward me, but simply to give me the best possible experiences. And so, if destiny markers and karma are created by the free will of my oversoul, and are thus beyond the free will of my current earth self, then the focus I choose to have, to influence life force as it flows in my life, is in the area left open to the free will of my current earth self.

In my experience, free will accesses a vast sea of possibilities, and I can use my influence to create probabilities. As I mentioned before, I love the work of Dr. Toni Petrinovich in *Divining Truth, Straight Talk from Source* as she provides the message of claiming the full power of who you are.[16] Using my influence of the fullness of who I am to attract probabilities allows me to take action rather than feeling like a cork bobbing in a river. I don't thrive in constant change when I feel like a cork bobbing in a river. I have discovered that I have a great

Chapter Four: Change Is Constant

deal of power within me with which to influence my reality. You have this same power within you. Everyone has the wisdom, the genius in themselves to do so, to become what she desires to be, and thus to create a resonant energy field of attraction. I continue working on developing mastery of influencing my reality in the area open to me to use my free will.

I began thriving in change when I chose to understand that I could not control things and I needed to stop believing and behaving as though I could. I also came to understand that there is no truth and there is no lie. There is simply a pattern of thoughts that form a belief. When I choose patterns of belief that produce useful and consistently useful results, I know I am developing myself in thriving in change. So I let go of my pattern of thoughts about controlling things. I adopted a pattern of thoughts that included seeing myself as a resonant energy field generator that could attract into my life what was best for my well-being. I adopted a belief of leading my life from a perspective that I have the blueprint for my optimal health inside me, as does every other organism, including organizations. I adopted a belief that genuine contact was a key to achieving results from the wholeness that I am. I adopted a belief that Spirit is all that is and that wonderful, tangible results come from working with Spirit. I can think of Spirit as conscious energy, and the results are the same. With these three beliefs replacing my previously held one about being able to survive only if I was in control of things, I had useful beliefs with which to forge ahead in my life in a way in which I thrive in change.

When I am not getting the results that feel good for my well-being, I do what I know to do to cleanse, balance, and nourish myself emotionally, spiritually, physically, and mentally. I work to be able to access my whole self, including these four dimensions of my consciousness. When I am cleansed, balanced, and nourished in these four dimensions of my consciousness, I show up in my life in the best shape that I can be in to thrive in constant change. From this foundation, I pay attention to influences around me that could cause me energy leakages, abandonment of my personal power, and any other ways that I might be lulled into sabotaging myself. I develop my conscious awareness of morphic fields so that I make conscious choices about the ones I do not want to align myself with and the ones that I admire and do want to align myself with. I am clear that I do not want to align myself with any morphic fields in which I could lose my power, in which people argue for their limitations, and in which people generate alignment with victimhood.

If I were to define this way of understanding how to thrive in change as a technique or method of some type, I would refer to it as a consciousness technology. In order to thrive in change, I shifted my consciousness. As an individual, thriving in change requires a shift in consciousness.

Note to self: thriving in change also requires a balance of action and rest. Rest more.

Your turn.

1. If what is conveyed here is true, what would I see?
2. If what is conveyed here is true, what would I hear?
3. If what is conveyed here is true, what would I feel?
4. If what is conveyed here is true, what would I know?
5. If what is conveyed here is true, how could this affect your leadership?

Notes

Organizations Thriving in Change

As you read this segment, to add experiences of your own, I invite you to reflect on

1. What color comes to mind?
2. What texture comes to mind?
3. What metaphor comes to mind?
4. What dance movement comes to mind?
5. What are you learning about genuine contact?

I wish I could give you reassurance that good organizational development techniques can result in an organization that thrives in change. The more likely picture is that organizations are built for stability. Traditional organizational development practice in the area of change management has been to discern the current state of the organization and to assist the organization to unfreeze from this current state. There is then activity undertaken to reach a predetermined desired state, with a refreezing of the organization at the desired state. The organizational development specialists agree that the mission was accomplished; if they are external consultants, they leave, and if they are internal consultants, they have a chance to witness what unfolds. The late Kathleen Dannemiller, a pioneer in examining this phenomenon with her Real-Time Strategic Change methodology, referred to organizations developing arthritic joints in which there was no flow of energy. Inevitably, the new locked-in state of the organization, like the previous state, ends up with arthritic joints causing great difficulties in the organization thriving in change.

Lawler and Worley, in their book *Built to Change,* note that ninety percent of change efforts fail.[17] They make the compelling case that a key hindrance to success with change is that organizations are built for stability and not for change. They strongly recommend that organizations be developed for change, emphasizing that the traditional organizational development practice of refreezing the organization at a new desired state does not provide the agility and flexibility that an organization needs. I would say that they are asking the professionals involved in organizational development to be willing to change.

I have worked with many organizations undergoing change, often in response to changes in their internal and external environments. I have observed two key ingredients that make all the difference in whether the change work is successful or not. The first is that the senior formal leader grasps the importance and impact of leading the organization to thrive in change, and is willing to lead the organization through the change process and to lead an organization that is flexible and adaptable. This requires the leader's capacity to embrace constant change and to create the conditions for the people of the organization to find their way in thriving with constant change. The second is that the individuals within the organization must take personal responsibility and work to thrive in change. Then, when the individuals come together as a collective, the capacity for the collective to thrive in change has the foundation it needs. Every time I have witnessed an organization that developed the capacity to thrive in change, both of these ingredients were crucial. Both key ingredients require a shift in consciousness. The first is for the formal leader shifting consciousness from ordinary leadership to extraordinary leadership. All leaders have this potential. The second is for the individuals in an organization to shift their consciousness from the current perception of ordinary reality to non-ordinary reality.

Accessing Collective Intelligence in Organizations

Thriving in change requires working with the collective of individuals that make up an organization. Whether the organization is the people who make up a couple, a family, a team, a department, or a whole organization, individual ability to thrive in change comes together into the collective ability to thrive in change. This collective ability often lies dormant in an organization because there is no forum for accessing the collective intelligence that is also made up of mental, emotional, spiritual, and physical dimensions of consciousness. The organizational breakthroughs that are possible from a shift in consciousness require the organizational capability of accessing the collective intelligence of those who make up the organization.

For years now, I have been intrigued by exploring collective intelligence and how to tap into the intelligence of a circle of people. I have been focused on this exploration for decades, believing in the power of the human capacity for finding solutions for the benefit of humanity, whether in a small enterprise or in global organizations. In the past I have witnessed organizations failing to thrive because the

Chapter Four: Change Is Constant

people worked in silos, lacking the organizational capacity to make use of collective intelligence in growth, regeneration, and innovation. The intelligence was there. I knew that the intelligence was there, because when people were out of their silos—for example, in the local pub after work—the solutions flowed as easily as the beer. They usually began with phrases like "If they would only listen to me," "You won't believe what *they* did now," or "If we had our way, we would be able to work more efficiently, but instead they have sent some expert to figure it out and *they* still aren't listening to us."

My exploration has taken me through an interesting journey that often challenged my previously held perspectives, causing me to discard patterns of thought and behavior and those perspectives that no longer fit for me. I have met fascinating people around the world, and no matter what country I am in, I meet people who are also questing to find solutions for a sustainable, regenerative, life-nurturing existence. These people have given me hope, because there are so many who are in this quest, and they seem to be located in every country.

I have learned the power of working with archetypes beginning with studying the work of Carl Jung. An archetype is a pattern that all humans have some form of resonance with, almost as though it is in their lived memories, even when it is not. When we lead our workshops, they are always conducted in a circle, with no tables or other barriers in between. In all countries, in all cultures, people thank us for bringing this format back to them and reminding them of their traditional way of working in a circle. The circle is a powerful archetype to assist people in remembering their wisdom.

In the 1980s I entered into a deep exploration of the Medicine Wheel of the indigenous peoples of the world, sometimes called the Gratitude Hoop or other names. In all indigenous cultures, there was a history of working in a circle divided into four quadrants in the directions of north, east, south and west, also a powerful archetype. Whether in ancient cave art or the later Medicine Wheel, this archetype was used to understand life and navigate to the unknown future as a community (organization) in order to develop an understanding of life, an understanding of community life, and agreed-upon solutions to navigate to the desired future of the community.

During the 1980s I also expanded my career from responsibility for public relations in one organization to achieving a life dream of becoming CEO of another organization. Both organizations were in the nonprofit health and social services sector. In my opinion, this is the most difficult sector to work in as a manager or CEO, because there are usually insufficient resources for the task at hand, a great will to do the job well, and the need to be versatile, adaptive, and yet stay on course. I believe that both the private and government sectors benefit when they hire people who have mastered leadership in the nonprofit sector.

I brought my learning with the Medicine Wheel into the organization, including the choice to have our staff meetings sitting in a circle. I did not get the results I was looking for, and so I sought the counsel of native elders on the nearby Six Nations reservation. I had worked with these elders for some years in the late '70s on matters having to do with the right of self-governance in relation to child welfare. At the time, I assisted in setting up the first child welfare agency on a native reservation in North America, run by native people for the purpose of attending to child welfare within the laws of Canada and also within the native culture. It was an end to the era of removing these children from the reservation and placing them in non-native foster homes and boarding schools, a practice that was abusive.

And so I went back to the elders. They listened to what I wanted to achieve in terms of transforming the organization that I was now responsible for, from a charity model to a social justice model, so that it could work more with our client base, side by side, showing respect for their dignity and right to make choices. I explained how I was bringing decision-making into a circle. They smiled and said, "Your heart and method are fine. The problem is that you hurry too much. When we have to find solutions, we take our time. We begin in a circle of chiefs, with the grandmothers standing behind. The chiefs must answer to the grandmothers and to the community they represent for their decisions. They understand that they have a lot of responsibility, not to their own egos, but to the grandmothers and to the community. And so, if it is not possible to find the right solution at one council, we wait until the next time there is a meeting. There is no shame in not finding the solution quickly. There is shame in not coming to the right solution for all who are affected." They then went on to tell stories of an annual meeting in which a solution might be sought for ten years in a row until all could come to agreement.

I said that I needed to find solutions quickly, and that the transformation to a different way of operating by our whole organization (community) needed to be achieved in a way that the new way of working and being was sustainable. They wished me luck, with smiles and words that told me that hurrying was inadvisable and would not give me the results I was looking for. It would have been easy at that point to give up on the way I wanted to lead the organization, to give up on working with my staff, board, volunteers, and community in a collaborative way that tapped into our collective wisdom.

I was also grateful to receive news in 1991 that it was time for the Medicine Wheel to be given by the red race to be used by the full human race. The red race had carefully preserved this knowledge for the human race for millennia so that it could again be used for creating a life-nurturing future for the human race. I am so deeply grateful for this gift to the human race. I recognize that not all native peoples are in agreement with this gift being used by the entire human race. I can only express my gratitude, and remember that at one time, we all had this knowledge. I am deeply grateful to the native peoples for preserving it, when the rest of us lost such knowledge.

Immediately upon this gift being released and my awareness of it, in rapid succession, I met Harrison Owen and learned about facilitating a meeting using his method of Open Space Technology (OST); I met the late Dr. Angeles Arrien and learned more about cross-cultural work with the Medicine Wheel in all indigenous cultures in the work she calls the Four-Fold Way, which transcends cultures; I met and learned from John Cobb about Process Philosophy and Process Theology,[18] which tied into what I knew about quantum physics; and I met and learned from Dr. Marge Denis from her work at the Ontario Institute for Studies in Education (OISIE) about facilitating meetings using Process Facilitation. All four advocated working with groups sitting in circles with no barriers between. That was encouraging for me. All four believed that there was a collective intelligence or collective wisdom that could be accessed, and that the solutions found could assist any group to achieve what might otherwise, in ordinary thinking, be deemed impossible.

Adaptive healthy growth requires that the organization has the capability to integrate the collective intelligence of everyone involved in the organization. It also requires that the means of accessing and using the collective intelligence is achieved by riding the waves of solutions rather than staying in the fixed, more limiting problem focus. Open Space Technology and Process Facilitation both provided methods for facilitating meetings that did not allow reality to be ignored, yet once reality was acknowledged, allowed people to use individual and collective intelligence to find solutions in a short time frame.

At the time, Open Space Technology (OST) meetings were two-day events, and later evolved to be successful in shorter time frames. I have no interest in how short a time frame eventually was achieved just for the sake of a short time frame. My interest lay more in how short a time frame would allow the use of collective intelligence in a way that was useful. My experience was that this could be achieved in a four-hour OST meeting, although to ensure that the best wisdom has emerged, I prefer meetings lasting two days or more. If it took a long time to get to the situation at hand—and in one case in one organization I worked with, the mess had existed for eighty years, costing them lots in time and money—then taking a full two to three days to find the solutions that could be successfully implemented by willing participants was a very small investment of both time and money.

Judging by the focus of people's thoughts and conversations, it seems to be harder to know what works than what doesn't work. The newly emerging field of positive psychology was formally birthed in the 1990s, highlighting that more than 90 percent of published articles in psychology were of something not working, with only a small percentage of articles focusing on something positive. Whether an individual is working on something in his or her life or organization, it is going to take a conscious and disciplined effort to shift from the tendency to focus on the problem to focusing on the solution. A number of books and other resources exist to assist individuals to shift what their mind focuses on for those interested in shifting from a problem-focused pattern of thinking to a solution-focused pattern of thinking. Yes, I am back to stressing the importance of the shift in consciousness of the individual.

In my explorations, I was interested in discovering whether such a shift in consciousness to riding the wave of solution rather than staying fixed in the problem is possible for the people that make up an organization. I was interested in the emergence of theories in the 1990s to do with critical mass thinking and the percentage of people required in a system in order to achieve a shift in the whole group. Various researchers found that if even ten percent of a group shifted their thinking and behavior, then the whole group could shift. The one significant proviso was that the group that made up the ten percent had to be representative of a maximum mixture of the organization. The same shift did not take place with only ten percent if that ten percent was all within one layer or grouping in the organization.

Critical mass thinking became a foundation for the emergence of a new stream of organizational development practice, sometimes referred to as Whole System Meetings and sometimes referred to as Large Group Interventions. OST was accepted as a credible, reliable method for leading meetings of the whole system and was considered the most open and, in my eighteen-year history with frequent use of OST, the most effective method for this new way of working to create shifts in organizations or collectives using the meeting as a catalyst. A shift from problem focus to solution focus in a collective was possible using OST and other whole system meeting methods. In my quest to assist organizations in benefiting from the wisdom of collective intelligence, it was important to be able to work with the collective in a way that the collective intelligence for solutions could be accessed quickly, even in a single meeting.

Ward and I as a team have the opportunity to work with extraordinary leaders around the world. Extraordinary leaders are able to do non-ordinary thinking and are willing to expand their perspectives. When we suggest to them that collective intelligence is a resource that they might want to pay more attention to, they understand the old adage that "the whole is greater than the sum of the parts" and they want to know how to make use of the collective intelligence of their organization so that their organizations have better results. We encourage these leaders to lead their organizations from a perspective that includes the development of a life-nurturing operating platform for their organizations, including a liberating structure and a participatory architecture, if they want to maximize the opportunities of working with the collective intelligence present in the organization.

The operating platform is usually the physical manifestation of the key formal leader's belief system of the organization, regarding how much freedom she is willing and able to give her staff to develop their own solutions and make their own decisions, and the framework she chooses to allow this freedom. How liberating can the structure be, so that people can actually get their work done efficiently based on their personal empowerment? She would need to be willing to command but not control. Command would include being very clear what her own nonnegotiables or givens are and what the degrees of freedom are for people in the organization to be innovative and to make decisions. In other words, she creates her own rules of engagement for the operations in the organization.

It is amazingly wonderful to watch the improvements in the organization when the rules of engagement and the operating platform are explicitly stated rather than having staff walk through a minefield of making assumptions about what is implicit in the operating platform. The beliefs of the leader and the liberating structure are two key ingredients of the operating platform. Another key ingredient is creating the time and space for highly participative meetings where the collective intelligence of those gathered for the meeting can be accessed. We refer to this as the development of a participatory architecture within the liberating structure.

Just as the individual needs to discipline her mind toward a solution focus—to avoid getting locked into a problem focus—the organization needs to develop its own discipline to do so. Within this discipline, there must be a pattern of using meetings and other forums to find solutions by benefiting from this often overlooked capacity of the organization's collective intelligence. In 1992 I began experimenting with frequent use of OST meetings to tap into the collective intelligence of the organization that I was responsible for. We had highly participatory meetings with good solutions emerging. In that respect, our use of OST meetings was highly successful for tapping into the collective intelligence. Our challenges were that the solutions kept running into barriers in our daily reality as an organization, and the energy for participating in the meetings started to wane as people discovered the problems in implementing their solutions. Fortunately, the staff size was about eighty, and we thus had the luxury to observe ourselves, our organization, and to look at this situation together and make adjustments.

We developed a liberating structure that began with me as the formal leader developing explicit nonnegotiables, which we called givens. I did not create these on my own but consulted with all the staff. This was a choice based on my style. Every leader has her own preference for discerning what is truly a given. We developed a way of working with OST in which we kept the facilitation of the meeting true to the teachings of Harrison Owen, yet we added work before and after the OST meeting to ensure that the results of the meeting had the highest likelihood of being implemented. For every OST meeting, we held a planning meeting, the OST meeting, a debrief meeting immediately after the OST meeting, and then a peer-to-peer accountability meeting about four months after the OST meeting. The entire process was facilitated using Whole Person Process Facilitation (WPPF) as a seamless container, with the insertion of the OST meeting into this container so that participants felt congruity.

The planning, debrief, and accountability meetings needed to be facilitated in a manner that was harmonious with the format of the OST meeting. I used what I had learned from Angeles Arrien and

Chapter Four: Change Is Constant

Marge Denis and developed WPPF for this purpose and to use in the organization when a more guided approach than OST was needed. Our participatory architecture included one whole system meeting using OST monthly, as well as team and division meetings using OST or WPPF for every meeting. With the use of these two participatory methods in an organizational operating structure that was liberating enough to allow participation, I found that we were able to tap into the collective intelligence of the people.

When we ran into the problem of creating so many solutions without the organizational capacity to work with the solutions, I realized that we needed to improve our operating platform as an organization to be able to achieve both short- and long-term benefits from the solutions and a means to hold ourselves accountable, as a collective, for the results. At the time, we were figuring out how an organization could benefit from collective intelligence to navigate in constant change. It was not a theoretical pursuit, but a living laboratory in which our board, senior leaders, middle management, staff and volunteers from our community consciously participated. I was fortunate to work with such a group, allowing for the learning when we tried something that worked and also when we tried something that didn't work.

The solution I came up with was to pose to the people involved the task of distilling key ingredients from the WPPF and OST meeting processes that could be extrapolated for use in the daily operations of the organization to create our operating platform. My thinking was that if extraordinary consciousness, behaviors and results could occur during one of these meetings, then borrowing key ingredients from these methods could achieve the same extraordinary results on an ongoing basis. One ingredient became the hub of the liberating structure in the operating platform—the Medicine Wheel. Harrison Owen had adapted the Medicine Wheel to apply to organizations.

He used this at the end of OST meetings to assist the participants to reflect on their performance during the meeting regarding leadership, vision, community, and management. He had used these four components of an organization, aligning them with the archetypes of warrior, visionary, healer, and teacher found in many versions of the Medicine Wheel. Over time, I developed and tested a way of working with the Medicine Wheel in a way that achieved sustainable results for the organizations I was working with. In the early days of this research I worked together with Dr. Larry Peterson of Ontario, Canada. Together, we published our findings in the February 1999 journal of *At Work: Stories of Tomorrow's Workplace*.[19] My research showed that the results of going through the Medicine Wheel were not sufficiently sustainable. As a result of my exploration and experimentation, I added three components and established an order that an organization needed to employ to develop an operating platform and to achieve sustainable results. The three additional components are purpose, relationships, and the circle of the whole. This became the Medicine Wheel Tool™ of the Genuine Contact program, with the trademark being for the process of how we use it, not for the Medicine Wheel itself.

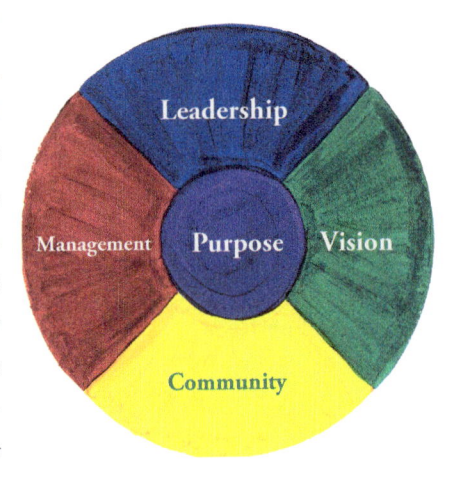

Following this evidence-based research, I used the framework provided by the Medicine Wheel Tool to provide guidance to the whole organization regarding the operating platform within which this participatory architecture would function. With this new operating system in place, we were able to triple our productivity, win awards for our quality performance, and do all this without increasing the tangible resources we used. We found solutions and we achieved an organizational transformation. All of this was done by working from the benefits of the collective intelligence within a life-nurturing operating platform. Using OST in our meetings was a significant cornerstone of our success.

By 1994, we referred to this as a Conscious Open Space Organization to highlight the importance of being conscious of the amount of open space in the organization. In 1995 I chose to follow my dream of being a full-time organizational consultant with my own business. I then set about the task of figuring out if I could achieve the same ability to thrive in change with optimal performance if I was not the formal leader. In other words, I wanted to find out if what we had achieved with an operating platform for an organization that included a liberating structure and a participatory architecture could be replicated in other organizations. Since that time, numerous organizations that we have worked with as consultants have experienced similar success.

By 1999 this method for working with organizations had developed into the Genuine Contact program, with our way of working with OST remaining a key ingredient.

I deliberately chose, and was fortunate to be contracted by, small to medium-sized organizations that wanted to benefit from their collective wisdom. Yes, they had extraordinary leaders. After several successful shifts in consciousness in organizations to achieve the desired breakthroughs, I was convinced that what we had worked out could be duplicated. In 1999, forming a life and business partnership with Ward, we created the Genuine Contact program so that we could teach this blended approach for working with organizations to others. In 2001, we had our first graduating class of people authorized to train others in our methods, with people from nine different countries. Today, we have many authorized trainers from many countries, most of whom work inside their own organizations. Some of them, however, do offer public training in the Genuine Contact program.

After a few years of continuous growth in the Genuine Contact program (GCP) and in the number of authorized trainers, Ward and I decided to open up the ownership of the GCP to a new co-owner model. We offered every authorized trainer the opportunity to join us as co-owners of the GCP and to support and guide the growth of the GCP in the world. We were pleasantly surprised that about forty trainers joined us in becoming co-owners of the program. Since then, the co-owners have created a leadership management team and have incorporated as a legal container for the Genuine Contact co-owners from which it can conduct business. It provides the leadership hub around which a membership organization can develop. The organization has the opportunity to conduct itself in ways that nourish a culture of leadership. It has been an amazing new organic model that is still developing and finding its way toward becoming an accepted model around the globe of how to best serve organizations in creating life-nurturing work environments with outstanding performance capabilities.

As co-owners of the Genuine Contact program, along with a number of the trainers, we work together in ways in which we endeavor to walk our talk with an operating platform designed to tap into our collective intelligence and to thrive in change. As a global organization that has participants in many countries, English is a common language, and yet for some of our members is a second or third language. We do not have the luxury of meeting in person as a whole organization, resulting in the need to find ways to operate true to our teachings in an online environment.

Chapter Four: Change Is Constant

Some of the members, led by Thomas Herrmann in Kungsbacka, Sweden, and Chris Weaver in North Carolina, USA, are developing our learning of how to do this well.

In 2007, we were honored with a chapter in *The Change Handbook*, an exceptionally well-done compendium of credible methods for accessing collective intelligence in organizations.[20] In 2008, I received concerns from one of our clients who had been a longer-term Conscious Open Space Organization. The original intent of being conscious of the amount of space that was open for accessing the collective intelligence was lost. The original intent had also included being conscious as an organization of the givens, identifying where space was not open in the organization for this purpose. Staff members felt that in a Conscious Open Space Organization, everything should be open. As a result of this concern, I examined the Conscious Open Space Organization and reported my findings to our professional community. We chose to make some adjustments in emphasis and renamed this type of organization as a Genuine Contact Organization (GCO), with the intention of reducing this misunderstanding and of focusing on our belief in the power of genuine contact in leadership and organizational development.

Note to self: I wonder if I can assist people in understanding that working with collective intelligence does not automatically mean working with a consensus decision-making model. I realize that this can be misunderstood.

Your turn.

1. If what is conveyed here is true, what would I see?
2. If what is conveyed here is true, what would I hear?
3. If what is conveyed here is true, what would I feel?
4. If what is conveyed here is true, what would I know?
5. If what is conveyed here is true, how could this affect your leadership?

Notes

CHAPTER FIVE

Keep It Simple

I Believe In Keeping It Simple

Simple frameworks and processes enable success with complex situations. Complex frameworks and processes get in the way of enabling success with complex situations. In keeping it simple, I recognize that any sustainable change must begin from the inside based on will, commitment, and determination.

As you read this segment, to add experiences of your own, I invite you to reflect on

1. What color comes to mind?
2. What texture comes to mind?
3. What metaphor comes to mind?
4. What dance movement comes to mind?
5. What are you learning about genuine contact?

In keeping it simple in my life, one of my favorite questions to ask is "Is this useful?" If it is useful, I work with it. If I don't feel it is useful, I quickly remove it from my focus. One way that I determine usefulness is to listen to whether I am feeling any sense of "I should do this" rather than a sense of "This is a useful framework or process for me to be successful, and I feel inspired to use it."

Addressing significant challenges for organizations and keeping it simple

On an ongoing basis, organizations today need to find solutions to complex problems in a very short period of time and then to rapidly implement the solution throughout the organization. They need to increase their capacity to navigate with change and take advantage of opportunities as they arise. Organizations need to have an operating system and a culture of leadership that retains good employees of all generations in which they feel inspired to work from their full potential.

In keeping it simple in organizations, I guide my choices from the five foundational beliefs of the Genuine Contact Way, stated simply as:

1. Spirit (conscious energy) is all that is.
2. All organisms have within them the blueprint for their perfect health. It is imperative that we learn to make life-nurturing rather than life-depleting choices.
3. Genuine contact with the self, one other, the collective(s), and all of creation is critical to our positive development and evolution both individually and as a collective.
4. Change is constant. We need to expand the capacity for working with constant change.
5. Simplicity allows us to handle complexity. We must keep it simple.

In keeping it simple, it is important to pause, slow down, and determine your beliefs in dealing with complex situations. You might even discover that these three beliefs are right for you too.

Within the conceptual framework created for me by these beliefs, I use highly participative meetings as a catalyst to move forward through complex situations. I have a lot of trust in collective wisdom, and because I believe that the blueprint for its optimal health lies in every organism, I trust that if people gather together in a meeting designed for maximum participation, success with complex situations will be found by the people involved.

In developing our Genuine Contact program, three meeting methodologies were chosen and developed that tap into the intellectual and intuitive wisdom of the individuals involved, and of the collective of stakeholders as a whole. The meeting methods used are simple, provide maximum choice and maximum freedom within a given context, and have a non-interventionist facilitation approach to ensure that the solutions have the space within which to emerge.

After identifying the three beliefs that provide a contextual framework for work with leadership and organizations, the use of highly participative meeting methods as a catalyst to work through complex situations, we also developed simple multipurpose tools and frameworks. The tools and frameworks are multipurpose, so that by learning each of them, it is possible to use the same knowledge and skills in multiple applications. Of equal importance, they are easy to duplicate and to learn.

After working with any combination of the components of the Genuine Contact program, people report to us that they had the organizational breakthroughs they were anticipating as well as additional breakthroughs they'd never imagined. The people involved as participants all come away with a level of knowledge about the basic tools that they can use over and over again.

People participate with this work in a number of ways, including: in workshops to learn a single module or the whole program; in organizations that use this work to find solutions to particular business goals; and, in organizations of all kinds that choose to use this work to develop their operating platform as an organization. Anyone who takes even one of the

Chapter Five: Keep It Simple

workshop modules receives the challenge of working on their genuine contact with themselves, with one another, with the collective, and with the Creator. For each of us, it is work that lasts for this lifetime, if we so choose. The desired outcome is to develop conscious and genuine contact with the essential self. This requires a shift in consciousness which working on genuine contact facilitates. It requires the awareness and engagement to claim one's leadership and to apply leadership first of all to one's own life.

The approach is affected by the commitment of Genuine Contact professionals to their own development in being in genuine contact and their recognition that it is an ongoing process that benefits from conscious awareness of the integration of ongoing learning. It is also affected by the capacity of the person to nourish a culture of leadership, beginning with self-leadership.

I have been asked if there could be tests for assessing the level of development in being in genuine contact and whether there is a way to assure leaders that the Genuine Contact professional they are working with has made sufficient advancement. I cannot do this. I also choose not to go down this path of measurement because I simply believe that Spirit is all that is, and so the organization will find a way to connect with exactly the right Genuine Contact professional who can be of greatest assistance at this point in the evolution of the organization.

Yes, the approach is also affected by the belief that Spirit is all that is, or conscious energy is all that is. Not all of the people who are Genuine Contact professionals or leaders who bring the Genuine Contact way into organizations believe that Spirit is all that is. The different belief systems about Spirit get in the way, as does the meaning of Spirit in different languages. From the beginning, I might have reduced confusion by saying Conscious Energy is all that is. I believe that all Genuine Contact professionals would agree with this or agree that there is some kind of force, as in "May the force be with you."

However Genuine Contact professionals work out their belief in some kind of force, I challenge them to ascertain whether the force is benevolent, neutral, or destructive. One reason for this challenge is that in our work we believe the wisdom to find the right solutions is always within the organism, just as is the blueprint for optimal health of the organism. This implies a benevolent, creative life force at work in all organizations, including in the entire human race. To be effective, those working with the Genuine Contact way need to develop themselves to be able to maintain this belief and not allow themselves to align with a sense of victimhood or fear.

If you try to change something from outside of an organization, resistance to the change emerges. It is natural. Imagine a person outside of an organization trying to shift the consciousness of an organization by making a plan and then planning to stick with the plan. I think you can imagine what the reaction would be if you were in this organization. As an organizational development consultant who works from outside of an organization, I am very clear that any work toward a change, including the shift in consciousness needed to thrive in change, must be led from inside the organization. I can provide tools and processes and then take on the role of teacher and mentor. I can neither lead nor manage the change.

Note to self: the next time I go through a personal change, I want to take notes and draw what I feel during the change process so that I can deepen my insights about change through a noticing exercise to expand my perception

Your turn.

1. If what is conveyed here is true, what would I see?
2. If what is conveyed here is true, what would I hear?
3. If what is conveyed here is true, what would I feel?
4. If what is conveyed here is true, what would I know?
5. If what is conveyed here is true, how could this affect your leadership?

Notes

Genuine Contact Tools and Frameworks

As you read this segment, to add experiences of your own, I invite you to reflect on

1. What color comes to mind?
2. What texture comes to mind?
3. What metaphor comes to mind?
4. What dance movement comes to mind?
5. What are you learning about genuine contact?

In designing the Genuine Contact program, we distilled the number of tools down to eight, using only simple tools that we could draw upon for multiple applications. Thus, we could teach a minimal number of tools to the people in the organizations we worked with so that the people themselves could use them when and where they identified the likely benefit in doing so. It was important for us to get our egos out of the way.

Our job is to be of service to those who engage us, to assist them and to focus on how to best meet their needs in a way that does not disempower them. We need to be willing to teach them what the tools are and how they can be applied. We need to understand that we are not there to offer something complex in order to show we are good as consultants. Complex frameworks and tools cannot assist people to handle complexity. Rather, simple frameworks and tools leave enough scope for people to deal with complex matters. So, simple tools that are easy to duplicate are taught. The tools are

1. Storyline
2. Deep Essence of the Organization
3. Cycle of Grieving and Healing
    (based on the work of Elisabeth Kübler-Ross)
4. Cycle of Transformation
    (based on the work of Amir Levy and Uri Merry)
5. Organizational Lifecycle
    (based on the work of Ichak Adizes)
6. Life-Nurturing or Life-Depleting Environment
    (based on work at the Ontario Institute for Studies in Education)
7. The Medicine Wheel Tool
    (based on teachings of the universal mandala of the four directions)
8. Givens

Storyline

The storyline allows us to look at what has happened in the past that has led up to our present situation. Looking at the past provides the opportunity to honor accomplishments as well as identify any events that need to be let go of in order to be ready to embrace the future. Looking at the future, even when developing a vision for the future, we are again working with story and could think of vision as the preferred future story we are choosing to shape our current activities. This tool is super simple and yet very powerful. People love telling stories in response to "What are the stories of this organization that led to this current event?" and "What are the stories that you have about the future of this organization?"

Deep Essence of the Organization

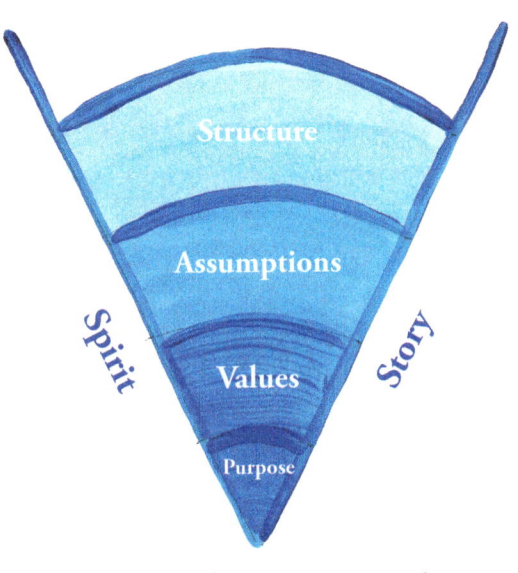

Often, when an organization is seeking change, they want changes in the behaviors and actions of the people, wanting some kind of behavior change process to be undertaken. Sustainable change requires working more deeply in the organization than at the surface level. Behaviors and actions are at the surface level. When working with the deep essence of the organization, we look at the underlying components that contribute to the behaviors and actions and make modifications at these deeper levels in order to realize change on the surface. To work with this Deep Essence Tool, imagine that it is a slice out of a sphere, with purpose in the middle, upon which everything else is developed. The story and spirit of the organization are radial arms in the sphere, influencing everything. Purpose is linked to behaviors and actions via values, assumptions, and structure.

Cycle of Grieving and Healing

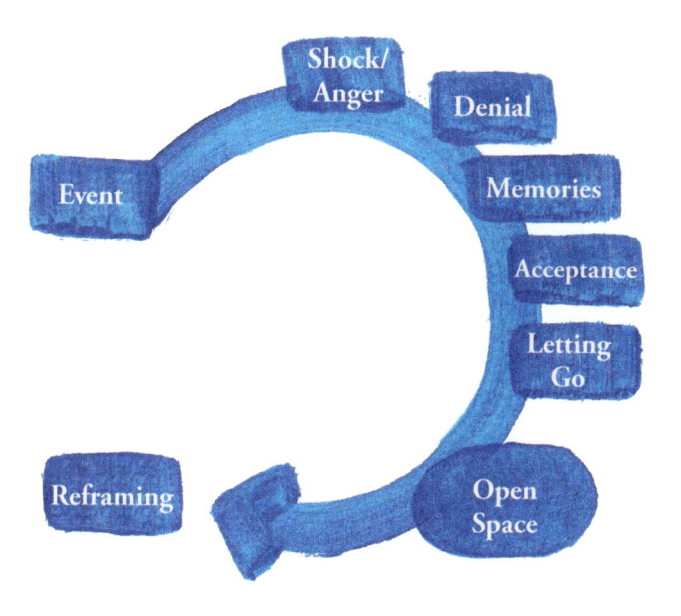

- Event
- Shock/Anger
- Denial
- Memories
- Acceptance
- Letting Go
- Open Space
- Reframing

Whenever an event happens, whether it is one we perceive as good or bad, it brings about change, and individuals and organizations will move through a fairly predictable cycle of grief and healing as a result of that event. Identifying where individuals, teams, and the organization as a whole are within their various grieving and healing processes provides insight into the most appropriate work to be done to assist the organization in moving forward. I have found that when everyone in the organization has been oriented to the effects of the grief cycle, the capacity to work with change increases as the shared concept and accompanying vocabulary provides an avenue for people to have important conversations. This increases the capacity for leadership.

Cycle of Organizational Transformation

Cycle diagram with the following labels (clockwise from top): Shock/Anger, Denial, Memories, Acceptance, Letting Go, Open Space, Reframing, Commitment, Planning, Training, Managing, Transitioning, Implementing, Stabilizing, Tune-Up, Development.

When an organization is seeking to transform itself, there is generally a predictable cycle of transformation that occurs. This cycle begins with the cycle of grieving and healing and then continues on to committing to the new way of operating and making the changes to get there. Understanding the cycle of transformation within the organization is another tool that increases the capacity to work with constant change as well as increasing the capacity for leadership.

Organizational Lifecycle

Most organizations follow a similar lifecycle pattern, from the conception of an idea through great growth toward peak performance, and then as bureaucracy sets in, slow stagnation toward death. It is, however, possible to sustain peak performance provided that the organization's operating system is designed to foster growth and development by paying attention to inspiration and creativity in relation to appropriate structure. Appropriate structure is just enough structure to support the inspiration and creativity sufficiently for it to be productive, while simultaneously continually minimizing structure so that the downward slide that comes from too much structure can be thwarted.

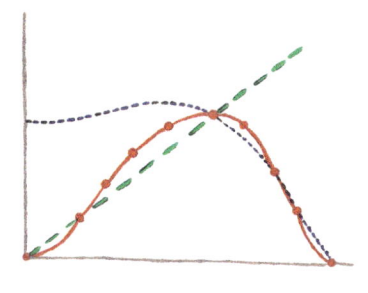

Life-Nurturing or Life-Depleting Environment

The environment within which people operate in an organization is key to the organization's success. Life-nurturing conditions contribute to high creativity, productivity, and job satisfaction, while life-depleting conditions contribute to low productivity and apathetic staff. Read the right-hand column of each diagram first and you will identify

These Kinds of Behaviors	Produce This Kind of Climate:	Resulting in these kinds of Response
• Listening • Understanding • Trusting • Sharing • Clarifying • Rewarding Appropriately • Focusing on Process rather than Outcome	**Life Nurturing**	• Experimenting • Creating • Exposing • Autonomy • Participating • Producing • Effectiveness • Efficiency

The Genuine Contact Way

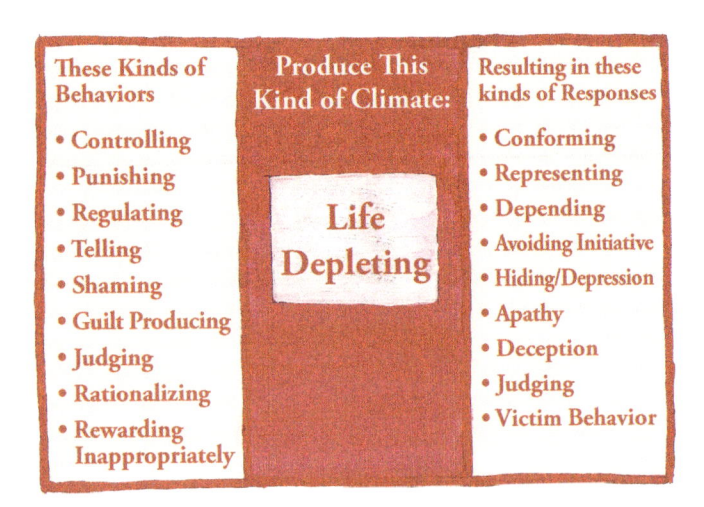

These Kinds of Behaviors	Produce This Kind of Climate:	Resulting in these kinds of Responses
• Controlling • Punishing • Regulating • Telling • Shaming • Guilt Producing • Judging • Rationalizing • Rewarding Inappropriately	**Life Depleting**	• Conforming • Representing • Depending • Avoiding Initiative • Hiding/Depression • Apathy • Deception • Judging • Victim Behavior

behaviors that are desirable, and others that are undesirable in creating a productive home or work environment. Now, read the left-hand columns of words that create either the life-depleting or life-nurturing environment. It is fairly easy to use this tool to do a quick assessment, and to develop a plan for altering the environment to get the behaviors that are desirable.

The Medicine Wheel Tool

The Medicine Wheel Tool is a simple framework to look holistically at an individual, organization, or project. As you navigate each part of the Medicine Wheel, questions are posed to come to a deeper understanding of that component. The questions will vary depending on the purpose and subject of the analysis. Once a cycle is completed, you can continue with another round. Each cycle expands understanding and offers further clarification of the questions. This tool is well suited for creating and then nourishing a culture of leadership.

Givens

To create the space for staff to be responsible, highly creative and innovative, solution-focused, and productive, the formal leaders need to be explicitly clear about the parameters of degree of freedom for creativity, innovation, and solution focus. Too often in organizations, these parameters or givens are implicitly communicated, resulting in managers and staff assuming that there are tighter parameters than truly exist. We use this simple tool to enter into conversations about the givens held by the senior leaders, testing and retesting whether what is stated is truly a given or whether it is open for change. This same tool can be used in a family when raising children, much as the earlier story by Rachel depicted. As she grew from childhood to young womanhood, the givens reduced regularly, continually giving her more space to take authority for her life. The tool depicts common categories of givens within an organization and can be adapted to other situations, such as for use within a family.

Genuine Contact Processes

Meetings, whether face-to-face or online, are the prime opportunity to create the shift in consciousness needed for organizational breakthroughs, including the collective breakthroughs needed for thriving in change. In order to achieve the desired results, meeting methods designed for maximum participation have the best results for whole system change. Good planning preceding the meeting, including asking people to attend a participatory meeting, is needed to determine what is to be achieved. The topic for the meeting should always be a business/organizational goal or challenge facing an organization for which solutions are sought. The significant organizational subject is a strong attractor field for people to access their creativity and find themselves using their collective intelligence.

There are a number of credible meetings designed for this purpose, with a wonderful summary of them found in *The Change Handbook* (second edition).[21] We recommend searching for methods that are right for your organization to achieve the benefit of using meetings to maximize the benefits gained from accessing the intelligence of the collective.

Because of my belief in the greatest possible benefits for our clients, I prefer meeting methods that create the conditions for participants to have maximum choice and maximum freedom. The maximum choice and maximum freedom that I advocate takes place within clear boundaries to define the amount of space within the organization that is genuinely open for participation and using the solutions generated.

Chapter Five: Keep It Simple

We stayed with the two simple processes of Open Space Technology (OST) and Whole Person Process Facilitation (WPPF) for conducting meetings designed for the purpose of benefiting from the collective intelligence. Our choice to include only two methods in the Genuine Contact program was in answer to wanting processes that could be used for multiple purposes and for multiple applications in organizations. This allowed us to teach a minimal number of processes in the organization that would meet the organization's needs to find solutions to business challenges. As an added bonus to finding solutions, the knowledge for facilitating the meeting methods developed as part of the capacity in the organization.

After some time, we realized that sometimes an actionable solution that would come out of an OST or WPPF meeting was to seek assistance in resolving a conflict. To meet this need, we developed Cross Cultural Conflict Resolution (CCCR) so that this method was available in the organization if it was needed. Descriptions of OST, WPPF, and CCCR can be found at http://www.dalarinternational.com/meeting-facilitation. Because both OST and WPPF often have conflict resolution occurring during the meeting process as a natural by-product, we rarely need to use the Cross Cultural Conflict Resolution meeting.

Open Space Technology

OST was developed by Harrison Owen, and yet within the Genuine Contact program we work with the method in a way that provides planning, the meeting itself, debriefing, and accountability components to optimize maximum long-term benefits.

Whole Person Process Facilitation

We created WPPF to have a method complementary to OST for use when a more guided approach is needed. We credit Marge Denis with her Process Facilitation work and the Ontario Institute for Studies in Education for providing the knowledge about how adults learn that is integral to WPPF.

Cross Cultural Conflict Resolution

CCCR is a conflict resolution method we developed based on our understanding of the conditions needed by all people, regardless of their culture. The work of Angeles Arrien greatly informed this process.

The Genuine Contact Organization

Each of the frameworks and processes within the Genuine Contact program can be used independently to achieve a specific purpose within an organization. All are designed to nourish a culture of leadership. Often, after an organization has seen the breakthroughs that are possible from using the frameworks and processes to achieve one purpose, they are eager to continue using this way of working toward additional goals. When the frameworks and processes are used in an ongoing and sustainable way, a Genuine Contact Organization begins to emerge.

I, along with my staff during the time that I was CEO of a multiservice health and social service, developed what we then called the first intentional Conscious Open Space Organization through a process of trial and error, synchronicities, and our conscious attention to our own process as we developed. A culture of leadership developed and prevailed that allowed us to work with triple the number of clients with the same number of staff, mobilize significant resources and public goodwill with an effective marketing campaign, and that allowed for continued innovation on the part of the staff to handle ever-increasing complex challenges of the inner city.

From this initial work with the Conscious Open Space Organization as well as almost two decades working internationally with organizations seeking a way of operating that could help them to achieve a culture of leadership, as well as greater and greater success, the concept of the Genuine Contact Organization (GCO) evolved.

The Genuine Contact Organization (GCO) is an organization that is highly successful in getting its work done, maintaining high staff morale, fulfilling its purpose, achieving its vision, and creating conditions and actions for new visions and their achievement. The GCO gets its business done in an effective and efficient way through its culture of leadership, achieving maximum benefit from the intellectual and intuitive knowledge of the individuals involved and of the collective. No two GCOs look alike. There is no model to follow to develop as a GCO because all organizations are organic and cannot fit into someone else's template.

There are, however, key focal points that are attended to: a holistic framework to operate within, principled leadership, and a different way of managing. Use is made of the frameworks and processes outlined in this chapter to enable the organization to choose what is right for it in every situation, relying on skills, knowledge, and capacity developed in-house and leading its own ongoing change from within.

All people within a GCO have the opportunity to achieve mastery of their work, both the regular tasks or work and individual or collective performance challenges. This mastery includes accessing intellectual and intuitive knowledge and the wisdom for applying it. In a culture of leadership, the people have an environment that supports their individual health and balance, resulting in less sick time off and better employee retention.

Within the GCO, a comprehensive blended approach within a holistic framework enables the organization to choose what is right

Chapter Five: Keep It Simple

for it in every situation, relying on skills, knowledge, and capacity developed in-house and leading its own ongoing change from within. Frequent use is made of Open Space Technology; Whole Person Process Facilitation; and when needed, Cross Cultural Conflict Resolution.

The GCO is an organization that is alive, aware, and chooses to nurture and strengthen its life for optimal performance. It allows the creation of the space needed for optimal accessing of its potential, possibilities, creativity, innovations, imagination, inspiration, insights, solutions, resolution, commitment, and focused action. It works from its strengths. It identifies and removes barriers. It sustains health and balance for the benefit of the organization and the people within it. If you have ever participated in an Open Space Technology meeting, it is easier to imagine the GCO, because it mirrors the same high performance that is experienced during an Open Space Technology meeting, but on a daily basis rather than just at an event.

In developing as a GCO, all participants in the organization become aware of the organization as one that is alive, nourishes a culture of leadership, is organic in nature, and is filled with untapped potential and possibilities. All participants become involved with developing the organization to have optimal performance through nurturing life rather than depleting life. Some of the development work that is necessary includes:

- How the organization is perceived by those who are involved with it and how it is consciously developed on an ongoing basis as it evolves and grows so that it can thrive in changing times. This includes a focus on health and balance.
- Identifying what works and how to strengthen it.
- Identifying what doesn't work and how to overcome it.
- Principled, spirited leadership leading in the chosen direction.

- A vision that is clear, focused, and achievable.
- How the individuals in the organization are perceived, treated, involved, held accountable, and rewarded.
- Changing leadership and management functions, including how authority, accountability, and responsibility are carried out throughout the organization.
- Changing structure, ensuring that "form follows function," so that the structure supports rather than hinders the effective work of the organization. Structure includes work and communications processes.
- Regular use of participative meetings. Participative meetings that are recommended include Open Space Technology, Whole Person Process Facilitation, Dynamic Facilitation, Appreciative Inquiry, and World Café.

Moving Forward

Forward

At the end of this book, it is time to look forward into your life, like looking through the windshield of the car to see where you are going. It is time to stop looking out of the rearview mirror, if that is the viewpoint you have taken to navigate your life. The windshield doesn't allow you to look too far ahead, and yet looking out the windshield from where you sit now is facing forward, getting on with your life and work.

I look forward to people everywhere embracing their courage and engaging in leadership of their lives. I trust that tips that you found in this book will help you to do so.

I look forward to people everywhere working to nourish a culture of leadership wherever they are involved in families and organizations of all kinds. Imagine if we changed our worldview to believe that leadership is everywhere, in everyone, and that we can create conditions in every organization we are part of for leadership to flourish and grow.

I look forward to people everywhere working on a shift in consciousness, individually and collectively, to create individual, organizational, and planetary breakthroughs to true wealth for all.

I look forward to people choosing the Genuine Contact way to provide inspiration to them to create a future that our grandchildren and all future generations will thank us for.

I look forward to the connections with those of you who choose to follow the Genuine Contact way more closely. Stay connected with us by going to www.genuinecontactway.com. Once there, you can find the opportunity to

- Sign up for the newsletter in which we share news, tips, and offers
- Sign up to follow us on our blog, Facebook, LinkedIn and YouTube
- Sign up for learning intensives in the Genuine Contact way and the Genuine Contact program
- Contact Birgitt Williams directly at birgitt@dalarinternational.com

If you are a leader, consultant, trainer, or facilitator and want to link with an international group of Genuine Contact professionals, here's how:

- Visit the Genuine Contact international website at: www.genuinecontact.net

Are you looking forward to being the change you want to see in the world? As you reflect on what you have learned during your reading and study of this book, what are you looking forward to?

Thank you for including the study of this book on your journey.

Birgitt

Namaste

Notes

1. Andreas Moritz, *Timeless Secrets of Health and Rejuvenation* (Enerchi.com, 2007).
2. The work was published in "The Toxic Handler: Organizational Hero—and Casualty," by Peter Frost and Sandra Robinson, *Harvard Business Review*, July 1999. http://hbr.org/1999/07/the-toxic-handler-organizational-hero-and-casualty/ar/1, accessed June 10, 2014. It's also in *Toxic Emotions at Work and What You Can Do About Them*, by Peter Frost (Harvard Business Review Press, 2007).
3. Guy Murchie, *The Seven Mysteries of Life: An Exploration of Science and Philosophy* (Boston: Mariner Books, 1999).
4. Walter Russell, *The Message of the Divine Iliad* (Waynesboro, VA: University of Science and Philosophy, 1971).
5. Angeles Arrien, *The Four-Fold Way: Walking the Paths of the Warrior, Teacher, Healer, and Visionary* (New York: HarperOne, 1993), 41.
6. Within this book, we have chosen to use the feminine form (her or she) for consistency and clarity.
7. R. D. Laing, quoted in John Edmonstone, *The Action Learner's Toolkit* (Gower Publishing, 2003), 3.
8. See http://explorersfoundation.org/glyphery/122.html. This poem by Marianne Williamson is in her book *Return to Love* (New York: Harper Collins, 1992).
9. Esther and Jerry Hicks, *Ask and It Is Given: Learning to Manifest Your Desires* (New York: Hay House, 2010), 114.

10. Ken Wilber, ed., *Quantum Questions: Mystical Writings of the World's Great Physicists* (Boston: Shambhala, 2001).

11. James Gleick, *Chaos: Making a New Science*, revised edition (New York: Penguin Books, 2008).

12. Richard Bartlett, *The Physics of Miracles: Tapping in to the Field of Consciousness Potential* (New York: Atria Books, 2010).

13. Itzhak Bentov, *Stalking the Wild Pendulum: On the Mechanics of Consciousness* (Rochester, Vermont: Destiny Books, 1988).

14. For more on Dr. Bruce Lipton and the biology of belief, see https://www.youtube.com/watch?v=jjj0xVM4x1I.

15. Candace B. Pert, *Molecules of Emotion: The Science Behind Mind-Body Medicine* (New York: Simon & Schuster, 1999).

16. Toni Elizabeth Sar'h Petrinovich, *Divining Truth: Straight Talk from Source* (West Conshohocken, PA: Infinity Publishing, 2012).

17. Edward E. Lawler III, Chris Worley, *Built to Change: How to Achieve Sustained Organizational Effectiveness* (San Francisco, CA: Jossey-Bass, 2006).

18. John B. Cobb Jr., David Ray Griffin, *Process Theology: An Introductory Exposition* (Westminster John Knox Press, 1996).

19. Birgit Bolton, Larry Peterson, "Open Space and Accepting the Benefits of Risk and Uncertainty," *At Work: Stories of Tomorrow's Workplace* Vol. 8, No. 1 (1999): 4–9.

20. Peggy Holman, Tom Devane, Steven Cady, *The Change Handbook: The Definitive Resource on Today's Best Methods for Engaging Whole Systems*, second edition (San Francisco, CA: Berrett-Koehler Publishers, 2007).

21. Ibid.

With Gratitude

I am grateful to everyone I have met on my life journey. Every person has helped me to understand the gifts of genuine contact, thereby assisting me in discovering who I am. My journey of genuine contact is blessed by my children Rachel, Laura, David, and Aaron. They showed me the way of love from the moment they were conceived in ways that I cannot describe in words. I am grateful to Ward, my life partner and business partner, who has brought so much into my life to allow me and us to expand and grow. I am grateful to my grandchildren, Jessica, Marleigh, Jaxson, and Leah. They are pure love, great teachers, and bringers of hope. I am also privileged to have an expanded family. Danny, Matt, Lily, and Christa have taught me the joys and growth that comes from being a bonus-mom. Others have joined the growing family, providing the fullness of what can be experienced from a blended family. I am grateful to each and every one for their contributions to my growth and understanding, and of course for their love.

I am grateful for all of the leaders and organizations that I have had the great privilege of working with and growing with. With you, I have had the opportunity to witness extraordinary leadership and the reality of life-nurturing organizations.

I am grateful that I have met, worked with, and played with the most incredible people around the world who are also committed to making a positive difference for ourselves and for the generations that follow. They reinspire me continuously. I am particularly grateful to those who have formed an international organization to support the work of the

Genuine Contact program getting out into the world, and I am grateful that this includes so many members of our family. I think of my friends and colleagues in Genuine Contact as members of our extended family and am grateful that they give of themselves, their hearts, minds, and souls to growing this work and knowledge in the world. I appreciate the collective desire to accomplish their shared vision of life-nurturing organizations in which people can thrive, and to leave behind a world in which people experience life-depleting work environments. I am grateful that together we continually figure out how to "walk the talk" of a culture of leadership. We took on a large challenge as we became a global organization quickly, needing to figure out how to be life-nurturing when most of our collaboration is done in an online environment.

I am grateful to my ancestors for passing on wisdom, experiences, and memories that helped me to grow.

I am grateful to my descendants that have not yet been born, as they are a large part of my inspiration to make a positive difference for the generations to come.

I am grateful to friends along the way—some who were friends for a season, others who are friends for a lifetime. Every one of you has enriched my life immeasurably in so many beautiful ways. Every one of you has influenced what is in this book, what I know, and what I teach. I acknowledge you here and in my heart.

Marianne Aal, Raffi Aftandelian, Lotta Alsen, Steven Alston, Christiane Amini, Angeles Arrien, Judy Arnott, Becky Arrington, Yetnayet Asfaw, Phil Assuncao, Tova Averbuch, Eiwor Backelund, Bhamathi Balasubrahmanyam, Ed Ball, Peter Bauer, Sainath Banerjee, Massee Bateman, Christoph Beck, Drew Becker, Christiane Bieker, Norma Bolton, Doug Bolton, Steph Bolton, Ann Boman, David Bonk, Deb Bonk, Matthias zur Bonsen, Juergen Bossert,

Sumana Brahman, Sabine Bredemeyer, Cia Brinkåker, Christian Buenck, Marquis Bureau, Maya Burkhard, Bev Carter, Sam Chan, Bonnie-Jean Chartrand, Kachina Chawla, Annick Chenier, Donna Clark, Ellen Cohen, Michelle Cooper, Maureen Corbett, Chris Corrigan, Marge Dennis, Naveen Devnani, Spenser Dresser, Ulrika Eklund, Monday Ekpa, Gabriela Ender, Gayatri Erlandson, Uwemedimao Esiet, Garrett Evans, Esther Ewing, Iyeshka Farmer, Marla Fera, Bettina Follenius, Cheryl Francisconi, Pape Gaye, Marianne Gerber, Diane Gibeault, Terry Gibson, Paul Gillooly, Philip Goodner, Doris Gottlieb, Theo Groot, Preeti Gujar, Barbara Hanna, Jim Hanna, Koos de Heer, Diane Henderson, Roxanne Henderson, Thomas Herrmann, Jutta Herzog, Ben Hewitt, Grant Heys, Joan Hicks, Monika Himpelmann, Brunhild Hofmann, Helga Hohn, Peggy Holman, John Hornecker, Peter Iorapuu, Sheila Isakson, Lyudmila Ivanova, Neeru Johri, Laureen Johnson, Duane July, Shaari Kamil, Sheila Keizer, Pat Kemp, Marai Kiele, Isabella Klien, Claudia Knapp, Elisabeth Teppler Kofod, Erich Kolenaty, Reinhard Kuchenmueller, Chitra Kumar, Manish Kumar, Shikhar Kumar, Sarine Labonte, Mark Lefko, Helene Lepire, Marta Levitt, Sara Lewis, Michael Lightweaver, Kerry Lindsey, Nancy Long, Caroline Lusky, Sylvia Machler, Bill Mackinnon, Susanne MacLachlan, Elena Marchuk, Lily Maresh, Gail Martini, Claire Masswohl, Myriam Mathys, Esther Matte, Maureen McCarthy, Tammy McCormick-Ferguson, Monica McGlynn-Stewart, Viv McWaters, Anne Merkel, Pierre-Marc Meunier, Joey Miquelon, Günther Morawetz, Debbie Morris, Madhuri Narayanan, Joan Nathanson, Zelle Nelson, Candy Newman, Michael Nothdurft, Janice Nutter, Abraham Nyako Jr., Denise O'Connor, Hope Oduma, Nancy Olivo, Denike Onasoga, Yemi Osanyin, Barry Owen, Debbie Owen, Harrison Owen, Emily Page, Sanjay Pandey, Michael Pannwitz, Michael Pannwitz Jr., Tripti PantJoshi, Gloria Parker, Laurie Parker, Kimberly Parry, Helen

With Gratitude

Patterson, Bharati Patel, Kriti Peters, Larry Peterson, Toni Petrinovich, George Philip, Kendra Phillips, John Pothiah, Jennifer Potts, Donna Price, Jipy Priscilia, Ernst Prossinger, Sharon Quarington, Anju Raheja, Andreas Reisner, Judi Richardson, Katrin Richter, Christl Riemer-Metzger, Judy Robertson, Rick Rocchetti, Birgit Rocholl, Sarah Rogers, Mary Rozenberg, Mary Rumley, Pitamber Sahni, Klaus Schessler, Richard Schultz, Marianne Sempler, Agneta Setterwall, Dykki Settle, Debbie Sexsmith, Mana Shah, Pradeep Sharma, Rubina Sharma, Vijay Prakash Sharma, Bockie Sherk, Rosemary Shovelton, Manju Shukla, Ashok Kumar Singh, Natasha Sinha, Michael Spencer, Anne Stadler, Lars Steinberg, Monica Stewart, Alan Stewart, Marianne Stifel, Constanze Stoll, Ingunn Svendsen, Eva P. Svensson, Rajiv Tandon, Elizabeth Tepper, Andreas Terhoeven, Andreas Tessendorf, Silke Tessendorf, Conrad Thimm, Margrethe Thømt, Anna Caroline Türk, Marina Tyasto, Vibha Kumar, Michael Vinson, Gwen Wagner, Catherine Walton, Bettina Warwitz, Dick Watson, Chris Weaver, Nancy Wells, Virginia Williams, Alyssa Wrenn, Aubrey Wrenn, Bailey Wrenn, Melissa Wrenn, Robbie Wrenn, Jean Wright, Roger Yomba, Mussarrat Youssuf, Ayalew Zegeye, Gernot Znidar, Liam Znidar, Sandra Znidar.

If I have left anyone out who feels that they helped me to grow in genuine contact, please know you are in my heart and that any omission from the list was an error on my part.

I extend gratitude to Bethany Kelly and her team at Courageous Creatives who carefully and gently assisted me in bringing this book to completion and out into the world.

And finally, my gratitude would not be complete without expressing my deep loving appreciation to the many helpers we have in other realms: beloved angels, ascended masters, guides, friends.

About the Author

Birgitt Williams is an international management and organizational solutions consultant, author, meeting facilitator, teacher, keynote speaker and executive coach. Her business focus is to create inspiring work environments that are highly effective in achieving their purpose and fulfilling their vision. She is an advocate of creating and nurturing a culture of leadership. Birgitt has mastery in possibility thinking and in working with the full potential of both tangible and intangible assets in organizations of all kinds, including private sector, public and government sector, communities, consortiums, and strategic collaborations. She is skillful at system change, team cohesion, strategy focus, multi-disciplinary teams, and cross-cultural work. Birgitt has devoted many years of her career to organizations that focus on newborn, child, and maternal survival and health.

Since 1999 Birgitt Williams (Birgitt) has been President and Senior Consultant of Dalar International Consultancy, Inc., of Raleigh, North Carolina, USA. Birgitt and her team specialize in developing leadership, developing organizations and teams, and developing consultants and coaches. Birgitt has demonstrated expertise in operational reviews, working at scale, team, organizational and community solutions, and organizational transformation, including in multidisciplinary and cross-cultural settings. Over the past seven years, her primary work has been with development agencies, the U.S. and city governments, and in the nonprofit sector in the field of health, particularly maternal, child, and newborn health and survival. She has worked with health care professionals, including researchers, in Nigeria, India, Indonesia, Australia, Ethiopia, the UK, Canada, Switzerland, Austria, the USA, Sweden, and Germany. She has been a mentor and executive coach to leaders and to senior organizational development consultants in Armenia, Australia, Austria, Cameroon, Canada, Finland, France, Germany, Israel, Korea, Netherlands, New Zealand, Nigeria, Norway, Russia, Sweden, Switzerland, Taiwan, UK, USA, Ethiopia, India, Nigeria, and Uganda.

Drawing upon her eclectic background in cognitive psychology, clinical behavioral sciences, organizational psychology, human services, health services, cross-cultural practices, biology, history, philosophy, and comparative religion studies, Birgitt is known and respected for her deep commitment, integrity, and her skills in facilitating positive and sustainable changes with individuals, teams, and organizations. As a professional and personal consultant, she brings a deep commitment, diverse and extensive experience, with a genuine, compassionate, and direct approach to her work. Her experience is drawn from her work with thousands of individuals and hundreds of organizations over 35 years.

Birgitt knew at the age of twenty-one that she wanted to be an organizational psychologist/consultant, working with systems. This awareness came to her during her first job after university, when she worked in a child welfare agency. She discovered that families who wished to better themselves and do right by their children were frequently prevented from doing so by the systems around them. That was in the days before systems theory was even talked about, but Birgitt made a commitment that she would become a consultant and work with systems as her life's work. She spent the next two decades preparing for this work, including taking postgraduate work equivalent to MA in a pilot program of clinical behavioral sciences that taught her about individual, couple, family, and organizational behavior, what interventions worked, what didn't, and why. During her two decades of preparation, she also took a number of training intensives to further develop her technical competency in various large group intervention methods to learn methods for creating change at scale, critical mass theory for organizations, participative processes to accomplish cross-sector collaborations and cooperation, and strategic planning, including focusing energy and work of strategic partners, strategic alliances, and consortiums. She has studied a number of modalities in the healing arts, achieving mastery in some.

Prior to becoming a leadership mentor and consultant to organizations, Birgitt insisted that it was important to have opportunity to lead an organization and to experience for herself whether all that she had learned about development, transformation, transition, and sustainability really worked when one was responsible and accountable for the performance of an organization. At the age of thirty-one, she had the good fortune to become the Chief Executive Officer of a multi-service social and health service organization. This period honed Birgitt's knowledge and skills from a senior leadership position, which has greatly and deeply enhanced what she brings to leaders, executives, and organizations in her consulting work. Birgitt offers simple but highly effective, powerful means of solving complex challenges. She believes that it is impossible to solve complex situations with complex means and that only simple means allow that which is complex to be dealt with. During this period, she developed principles from which she works.

CPSIA information can be obtained at www.ICGtesting.com
Printed in the USA
LVOW02s0319021114

410930LV00002B/2/P